WAR, PEACE AND SOCIAL CHANGE:
EUROPE 1900–1955

DOCUMENTS 1: 1900–1929

This collection is one part of an Open University integrated teaching system and the selection is therefore related to other material available to students. It is designed to evoke the critical understanding of students.

A318 War, Peace and Social Change: Europe 1900–1955

Book I Europe on the Eve of War 1900–1914

Book II World War I and Its Consequences

Book III Between Two Wars

Book IV World War II and Its Consequences

Book V War and Change in Twentieth-Century Europe

Prepared by the course team and published by the Open University Press, 1990

Other material associated with the course

Documents 1:1900–1929, eds Arthur Marwick and Wendy Simpson, Open University Press, 1990

Documents 2: 1925–1959, eds Arthur Marwick and Wendy Simpson, Open University Press, 1990
War, Peace and Social Change in Twentieth-Century Europe, eds Clive Emsley, Arthur Marwick and Wendy Simpson, Open University Press, 1990 (Course Reader)

Europe 1880–1945, J. M. Roberts, Longman, 1989 (second edition) (set book)

If you are interested in studying the course, contact the Student Enquiries Office, The Open University, PO Box 71, Milton Keynes MK7 6AG.

Cover illustration: 'U-boats out!' (Trustees of the Imperial War Museum)

WAR, PEACE AND SOCIAL CHANGE:
EUROPE 1900–1955

DOCUMENTS 1: 1900–1929

Edited by Arthur Marwick and Wendy Simpson

**OPEN
UNIVERSITY
PRESS**

Open University Press
in association with
The Open University

The Open
University

Open University Press
Celtic Court
Buckingham
MK18 1XT

and
1900 Frost Road, Suite 101
Bristol, PA 19007, USA

First Published 1990

British Library Cataloguing in Publication Data

War, peace and social change: Europe 1900–1955.—(A318)
    Documents 1.
    1. Europe, history
    I. Marwick, Arthur, *1936–*   II. Simpson, Wendy   III. Open
    University, *A318 war, peace and social change course team*
    IIII. Open University
    940

    ISBN 0 335 09301 9
    ISBN 0 335 09300 0 (pbk)

Library of Congress Cataloging-in-Publication Data

War, peace and social change—Europe c. 1900–c. 1955: documents/
    edited by Arthur Marwick and Wendy Simpson.
       p. cm.
    Material associated with Open University Course A318 War, peace
    and social change—Europe c. 1900–c. 1955.
       Contents: Contents: v. 1. Documents 1, 1900–1929.
       ISBN 0-335-09301-9. — ISBN 0-335-09300-0 (pbk.)
       1. World War, 1914–1918—Causes—Sources.   2. World War,
    1914–1918—Influence—Sources.   3. World War, 1939–1945—Causes–
    –Sources.   4. World War, 1939–1945—Influence—Sources.   5. Europe–
    –Social conditions—20th century—Sources.   6. Social change–
    –History—20th century—Sources.   I. Marwick, Arthur, 1936–
    II. Simpson, Wendy, 1941–
    D521.W33   1990
    940.2—dc20   89-23127 CIP

Typeset by Rowland Phototypesetting Ltd,
Bury St Edmunds, Suffolk
Printed in Great Britain by
St Edmundsbury Press Ltd,
Bury St Edmunds, Suffolk

PREFACE

Primary sources – or documents as they were called before the great expansion from the traditional, purely written sources to all kinds of visual and non-traditional sources – are the raw material of history. The subject of war, peace and social change, an absolutely essential one in the study of twentieth-century European history, gives rise to many vigorous debates. Did the wars have significant social consequences? What is the relationship between the First World War and the Russian, Austrian and German revolutions? Do wars lower or improve the status of women? What is the relationship between war and the arts? Did total war produce mass society, or was mass society produced by total war?

These debates can be followed in the writings of historians, but they should also be studied from the primary sources. In all their variety – and in this book are reproduced extracts from diaries, social surveys, acts of parliament, international treaties, novels and poems, newspaper reports, and texts taken from many different countries – primary sources bring one directly into contact with the real texture of history.

This collection, together with its companion volume *Documents 2: 1925–1959*, is designed to accompany the Open University course A318 *War, Peace and Social Change: Europe 1900–1955*, but it will prove of immense value to anyone interested in twentieth-century European history, over which two cataclysmic wars have had a profound influence, and especially to anyone with a particular interest in social history.

The documents in this volume have been divided into two sections, which correspond to the first two books of the course. Section I covers the period up to 1914, while Section II covers the period of the First World War and its aftermath. Although the documents are of many types and relate to many different topics – political, economic, diplomatic and cultural, as well as social – there is no sub-organization within these sections. Indeed, the documents have been arranged in the order in which they are used within the Open University course. This means that they can be approached without any deep preconceptions about which particular topic any of the texts relates to. In fact, depending on the questions asked, primary sources can suggest an amazing range of answers. This method of ordering the documents also results in some fascinating juxtapositions – poems with acts of parliament, personal reminiscences with international treaties.

The documents have been selected (and sometimes translated) by members of the course team responsible for *War, Peace and Social Change*.

ARTHUR MARWICK
WENDY SIMPSON

ACKNOWLEDGEMENTS

Grateful acknowledgement is made to the following sources for material used in this volume:

I.16: Extract taken from *The History of the British Film 1906–1914*, by Rachael Lowe reproduced by kind permission of Unwin Hyman Ltd. ©; *I.17*: S. B. Clough and S. Saladine (eds) *A History of Modern Italy: Documents, Reading and Commentary*, Columbia University Press, 1968; *I.18, I.19 and I.20*: Basil Dmytryshyn (ed.) *Imperial Russia, A Source Book 1900–1917*, The Dryden Press, 1974; *I.21*: Vernon L. Lidtke, *The Outlawed Party: Social Democracy in Germany, 1878–1890*. Copyright © 1966 by Princeton University Press. Excerpt pp. 335–338 reprinted with permission of Princeton University Press; *I.24 and I.25*: David Thompson, *France: Empire and Republic 1850–1940*. Copyright © 1968 by David Thompson. Reprinted by permission of Walker and Company; *II.1*: Louis L. Snyder (ed.) *Historic Documents of World War I*, Van Nostrand Reinhold Co., 1958; *II.7*: J-J. Becker, *The Great War and the French People*, Berg Publishers Ltd., 1985; *II.14*: Henri Barbusse, *Under Fire*, trans. W. Fitzwater Wray, © J. M. Dent & Sons Ltd., 1965; E. M. Remarque, *All Quiet on the Western Front*, trans. A. W. Wheen, The Bodley Head/Little Brown Inc., 1929, © the Estate of E. M. Remarque; *II.16, II.17, II.18, II.19, II.20 and II.21*: G. Vernadsky *et al.* (eds) *A Source Book for Russian History from Early Times to 1917*, vol. 3. Copyright © 1972 Yale University Press; *II.22 and II.23*: Paul Avrich, *Kronstadt 1921*. Copyright © 1970 by Princeton University Press; *II.25*: Hans Peter Hanssen, *Diary of a Dying Empire*, trans. Oscar Osburn Winther, © 1955 Indiana University Press; *II.26*: Z. A. B. Zeman, *The Break-Up of the Habsburg Empire 1914–1918: A Study in National and Social Revolution*, © 1961 Oxford University Press.

CONTENTS

I Europe on the Eve of War 1900–1914

II World War I and Its Consequences

I
EUROPE ON THE EVE OF WAR
1900–1914

I.1 'Dominance of Russia or Germany', letter to *The Times* (1 Aug. 1914)

VIEWS OF MR NORMAN ANGELL TO THE EDITOR OF THE TIMES

Sir, – A nation's first duty is to its own people.

We are asked to intervene in the Continental war because unless we do so we shall be 'isolated'. The isolation which will result for us if we keep out of this war is that, while other nations are torn and weakened by war, we shall not be, and by that fact might conceivably for a long time be the strongest Power in Europe, and, by virtue of our strength and isolation, its arbiter, perhaps, to useful ends.

We are told that if we allow Germany to become victorious she would be so powerful as to threaten our existence by the occupation of Belgium, Holland, and possibly the North of France. But, as your article of to-day's date so well points out, it was the difficulty which prevented her from acting against us during the South African War. If one province, so largely German in its origin and history, could create this embarrassment, what trouble will not Germany pile up for herself if she should attempt the absorption of a Belgium, a Holland, and a Normandy? She would have created for herself embarrassments compared with which Alsace and Poland would be a trifle: and Russia, with her 160,000,000, would in a year or two be as great a menace to her as ever.

The object and effect of our entering into this war would be to ensure the victory of Russia and her Slavonic allies. Will a dominant Slavonic federation of, say, 200,000,000 autocratically governed people, with a very rudimentary civilization, but heavily equipped for military aggression, be a less dangerous factor in Europe than a dominant Germany of 65,000,000,000 highly civilized and mainly given to the arts of trade and commerce? ·

The last war we fought on the Continent was for the purpose of preventing the growth of Russia. We are now asked to fight one for the purpose of promoting it. It is now universally admitted that our last Continental war – the Crimean War – was a monstrous error and miscalculation. Would this intervention be any wiser or likely to be better in its results?

On several occasions Sir Edward Gray has solemnly declared to support France, and there is certainly no moral obligation on the part of the English people so to do. We can best serve civilization, Europe – including France – and ourselves by remaining the one power in Europe that has not yielded to war madness.

This, I believe, will be found to be the firm conviction of the overwhelming majority of the English people.

Yours faithfully,

Norman Angell
4, King's Bench-Walk, Temple, E.C., July 31.   (*The Times*, 1 August 1914)

I.2 'Scholars' protest against war with Germany', from *The Times* (1 Aug. 1914)

Peace manifestos were issued from various quarters yesterday. A number of University professors and others, who state that they all in different ways enjoy the friendship and co-operation of German colleagues, sign the following protest and appeal for the support of English scholars:

We regard Germany as a nation leading the way in the Arts and Sciences, and we have all learnt and are learning from German scholars. War upon her in the interest of Serbia and Russia will be a sin against civilization. If by reason of honourable obligations we be unhappily involved in war, patriotism might still our mouths, but at this juncture we consider ourselves justified in protesting against being drawn into the struggle with a nation so near akin to our own, and with whom we have so much in common.

(*The Times*, 1 August 1914)

I.3 'A socialist demonstration', from *The Times* (1 Aug. 1914)

The Socialists decided at a meeting at the House of Commons yesterday to hold a demonstration in Trafalgar-square to-morrow. A resolution similar in terms to one passed by the British section of the International Socialist Bureau, under the chairmanship of Mr Keir Hardie, will be moved at the meeting. That resolution is in the following terms:

That we view with serious alarm the prospect of a European war into which every European power will be dragged owing to secret alliances and understandings which, in their origin, were never sanctioned by the nations, nor are even now communicated to them.

We stand by the efforts of the international working class movement to unite the workers of the nations concerned in their efforts to prevent their Governments from entering upon war, as expressed in the resolution passed by the International Socialist Bureau.

We protest against any step being taken by the Government of this country to support Russia, either directly or in consequence of any understanding with France as being not only offensive to the political traditions of the country but disastrous to Europe, and declare that as we have no interest, direct or indirect, in the threatened quarrels which may result from the action of Austria in Serbia, the Government of Great Britain should decline to engage in war, but should confine itself to efforts to bring about peace as speedily as possible.

(*The Times*, 1 August 1914)

I.4   A. H. Hobson, 'Economic parasites of imperialism' (1903)

Seeing that the Imperialism of the last three decades is clearly condemned as a business policy, in that at enormous expense it has procured a small, bad, unsafe increase of markets, and has jeopardised the entire wealth of the nation in rousing the strong resentment of other nations, we may ask, 'How is the British nation induced to embark upon such unsound business?' The only possible answer is that the business interests of the nation as a whole are subordinated to those of certain sectional interests that usurp control of the national resources and use them for their private gain. This is no strange or monstrous charge to bring; it is the commonest disease of all forms of government. The famous words of Sir Thomas More are as true now as when he wrote them: 'Everywhere do I perceive a certain conspiracy of rich men seeking their own advantage under the name and pretext of the commonwealth.'

Although the new Imperialism has been bad business for the nation, it has been good business for certain classes and certain trades within the nation. The vast expenditure on armaments, the costly wars, the grave risks and embarrassments of foreign policy, the stoppage of political and social reforms within Great Britain, though fraught with great injury to the nation, have served well the present business interests of certain industries and professions.

It is idle to meddle with politics unless we clearly recognise this central fact and understand what these sectional interests are which are the enemies of national safety and the commonwealth. We must put aside the merely sentimental diagnosis which explains wars or other national blunders by outbursts of patriotic animosity or errors of statecraft. Doubtless at every outbreak of war not only the man in the street but the man at the helm is often duped by the cunning with which aggressive motives and greedy purposes dress themselves in defensive clothing. There is, it may be safely asserted, no war within memory, however nakedly aggressive it may seem to the dispassionate historian, which has not been presented to the people who were called upon to fight as a necessary defensive policy, in which the honour, perhaps the very existence, of the State was involved.

The disastrous folly of these wars, the material and moral damage inflicted even on the victor, appear so plain to the disinterested spectator that he is apt to despair of any State attaining years of discretion, and inclines to regard these natural cataclysms as implying some ultimate irrationalism in politics. But careful analysis of the existing relations between business and politics shows that the aggressive Imperialism which we seek to understand is not in the main the product of blind passions of races or of the mixed folly and ambition of politicians. It is far more rational than at first sight appears. Irrational from the standpoint of the whole nation, it is rational enough from the standpoint of certain classes in the nation. A completely socialist State which kept good books and presented regular balance-sheets of expenditure and assets would soon discard Imperialism; an intelligent *laissez-faire* democracy which gave duly proportionate weight in its policy to all economic interests alike would do the same. But a State in which certain well-organised business interests are able to outweigh the weak, diffused interest of the community is bound to pursue a policy which accords with the pressure of the former interests.

In order to explain Imperialism on this hypothesis we have to answer two questions. Do we find in Great Britain to-day any well-organised group of special commercial and social interests which stand to gain by aggressive Imperialism and the militarism it involves? If such a combination of interests exists, has it the power to work its will in the arena of politics?

What is the direct economic outcome of Imperialism? A great expenditure of public money upon ships, guns, military and naval equipment and stores, growing and productive of enormous profits when a war, or an alarm of war, occurs; new public loans and important fluctuations in the home and foreign Bourses; more posts for soldiers and sailors and in the diplomatic and consular services; improvement of foreign investments by the substitution of the British flag for a foreign flag; acquisition of markets for certain classes of exports, and some protection and assistance for trades representing British houses in these manufactures; employment for engineers, missionaries, speculative miners, ranchers and other emigrants.

Certain definite business and professional interests feeding upon imperialistic expenditure, or upon the results of that expenditure, are thus set up in opposition to the common good, and, instinctively feeling their way to one another, are found united in strong sympathy to support every new imperialist exploit.

If the £60,000,000 which may now be taken as a minimum expenditure on armaments in time of peace were subjected to a close analysis, most of it would be traced directly to the tills of certain big firms engaged in building warships and transports, equipping and coaling them, manufacturing guns, rifles, and ammunition, supplying horses, waggons, saddlery, food, clothing for the services, contracting for barracks, and for other large irregular needs. Through these main channels the millions flow to feed many subsidiary trades, most of which are quite aware that they are engaged in executing contracts for the services. Here we have an important nucleus of commercial Imperialism. Some of these trades, especially the shipbuilding, boiler-making, and gun and ammunition making trades, are conducted by large firms with immense capital, whose heads are well aware of the uses of political influence for trade purposes.

These men are Imperialists by conviction; a pushful policy is good for them.

With them stand the great manufacturers for export trade, who gain a living by supplying the real or artificial wants of the new countries we annex or open up. Manchester, Sheffield, Birmingham, to name three representative cases, are full of firms which compete in pushing textiles and hardware, engines, tools, machinery, spirits, guns, upon new markets. The public debts which ripen in our colonies, and in foreign countries that come under our protectorate or influence, are largely loaned in the shape of rails, engines, guns, and other materials of civilisation made and sent out by British firms. The making of railways, canals, and other public works, the establishment of factories, the development of mines, the improvement of agriculture in new countries, stimulate a definite interest in important manufacturing industries which feeds a very firm imperialist faith in their owners.

The proportion which such trade bears to the total industry of Great Britain is very small, but some of it is extremely influential and able to make a definite impression upon politics, through chambers of commerce, Parliamentary representatives, and semi-political, semi-commercial bodies like the Imperial South African Association or the China League.

The shipping trade has a very definite interest which makes for Imperialism. This is well illustrated by the policy of State subsidies now claimed by shipping firms as a retainer, and in order to encourage British shipping for purposes of imperial safety and defence.

The services are, of course, imperialist by conviction and by professional interest, and every increase of the army and navy enhances their numerical strength and the political power they exert. The abolition of purchase in the army, by opening the profession to the upper middle classes, greatly enlarged this most direct feeder of imperial sentiment. The potency of this factor is, of course, largely due to the itch for glory and adventure among military officers upon disturbed or uncertain frontiers of the Empire. This has been a most prolific source of expansion in India. The direct professional influence of the services carries with it a less organised but powerful sympathetic support on the part of the aristocracy and the wealthy classes, who seek in the services careers for their sons.

To the military services we may add the Indian Civil Service and the numerous official and semi-official posts in our colonies and protectorates. Every expansion of the Empire is also regarded by these same classes as affording new openings for their sons as ranchers, planters, engineers, or missionaries. This point of view is aptly summarised by a high Indian official, Sir Charles Crossthwaite, in discussing British relations with Siam. 'The real question was who was to get the trade with them, and how we could make the most of them, so as to find fresh markets for our goods and also employment for those superfluous articles of the present day, our boys.'

From this standpoint our colonies still remain what James Mill cynically described them as being, 'a vast system of outdoor relief for the upper classes.'

In all the professions, military and civil, the army, diplomacy, the church, the bar, teaching and engineering, Greater Britain serves for an overflow, relieving the congestion of the home market and offering chances to more reckless or adventurous members, while it furnishes a convenient limbo for damaged characters and careers. The actual amount of profitable employment thus furnished by our recent acquisitions is inconsiderable, but it arouses that disproportionate interest which always attaches to the margin of employment. To extend this margin is a powerful motive in Imperialism.

These influences, primarily economic, though not unmixed with other sentimental motives, are particularly operative in military, clerical, academic, and Civil Service circles, and furnish an interested bias towards Imperialism throughout the educated classes.

(*Imperialism*, Nisbet, 1903, pp. 51–6)

I.5 A. H. Hobson, 'The economic taproot of imperialism' (1903)

Over-production in the sense of an excessive manufacturing plant, and surplus capital which cannot find sound investments within the country, force Great Britain, Germany, Holland, France to place larger and larger portions of their economic resources outside the area of their present political domain, and then stimulate a policy of political expansion so as to take in the new areas. The economic sources of this movement are laid bare by periodic trade-depressions due to an inability of producers to find adequate and profitable markets for what they can produce. The Majority Report of the Commission upon the Depression of Trade in 1885 put the matter in a nut-shell. 'That, owing to the nature of the times, the demand for our commodities does not increase at the same rate as formerly; that our capacity for production is consequently in excess of our requirements, and could be considerably increased at short notice; that this is due partly to the competition of the capital which is being steadily accumulated in the country.' The Minority Report straightly imputes the condition of affairs to 'over-production'. Germany is at the present time suffering severely from what is called a glut of capital and of manufacturing power: she must have new markets; her Consuls all over the world are 'hustling' for trade; trading settlements are forced upon Asia Minor; in East and West Africa, in China and elsewhere the German Empire is impelled to a policy of colonization and protectorates as outlets for German commercial energy.

Every improvement of methods of production, every concentration of ownership and control, seems to accentuate the tendency. As one nation after another enters the machine economy and adopts advanced industrial methods, it becomes more difficult for its manufacturers, merchants, and financiers to dispose profitably of their economic resources, and they are tempted more and more to use their Governments in order to secure for their particular use some distant undeveloped country by annexation and protection.

The process we may be told is inevitable, and so it seems upon a superficial inspection. Everywhere appear excessive powers of production, excessive capital in search of investment. It is admitted by all business men that the growth of the powers of production in their country exceeds the growth in consumption, that more goods can be produced than can be sold at a profit, and that more capital exists than can find remunerative investment.

It is this economic condition of affairs that forms the taproot of Imperialism. If the consuming public in this country raised its standard of consumption to keep pace with every rise of productive powers, there could be no excess of goods or capital clamorous to use Imperialism in order to find markets: foreign trade would indeed exist, but there would be no difficulty in exchanging a small surplus of our manufactures for the food and raw material we annually absorbed, and all the savings that we made could find employment, if we chose, in home industries.

There is nothing inherently irrational in such a supposition. Whatever is, or can be, produced, can be consumed, for a claim upon it, as rent, profit, or wages, forms part of the real income of some member of the community, and he can consume it, or else exchange it for some other consumable with some one else who will consume it. With everything that is produced a consuming power is born. If then there are goods which cannot get consumed, or which cannot even get produced because it is evident they cannot get consumed, and if there is a quantity of capital and labour which cannot get full employment because its products cannot get consumed, the only possible explanation of this paradox is the refusal of owners of consuming power to apply that power in effective demand for commodities.

It is, of course, possible that an excess of producing power might exist in particular industries by misdirection, being engaged in certain manufactures, where it ought to have been engaged in agriculture or some other use. But no one can seriously contend that such misdirection explains the recurrent gluts and consequent depressions of modern industry, or that, when over-production is manifest in the leading manufactures, ample avenues are open for the surplus capital and labour in other industries. The general character of the excess of producing power is proved by the existence at such times of large bank stocks of idle money seeking any sort of profitable investment and finding none.

The root questions underlying the phenomena are clearly these: 'Why is it that consumption fails to keep pace automatically in a community with power of production?' 'Why does under-consumption or over-saving occur?' For it is evident that the consuming power, which, if exercised, would keep tense the reins of production, is in part withheld, or in other words is 'saved' and stored up for investment. All saving for investment does not imply slackness of production; quite the contrary. Saving is economically justified, from the social standpoint, when the capital in which it takes material shape finds full employment in helping to produce commodities which, when produced, will be consumed. It is saving in excess of this amount that causes mischief, taking shape in surplus capital which is not needed to assist current consumption, and which either lies idle, or tries to oust existing capital from its employment, or else seeks speculative use abroad under the protection of the Government.

But it may be asked, 'Why should there be any tendency to over-saving? Why should the owners of consuming power withhold a larger quantity for savings than can be serviceably employed?' Another way of putting the same question is this, 'Why should not the pressure of present wants keep pace with every possibility of satisfying them?' The answer to these pertinent questions carries us to the broadest issue of the distribution of wealth. If a tendency to distribute income or consuming power according to needs were operative, it is evident that consumption would rise with every rise of producing power, for human needs are illimitable, and there could be no excess of saving. But it is quite otherwise in a state of economic society where distribution has no fixed relation to needs, but is determined by other conditions which assign to some people a consuming power vastly in excess of needs or possible uses, while others are destitute of consuming power enough to satisfy even the full demands of physical efficiency.

Thus we reach the conclusion that Imperialism is the endeavour of the great controllors of industry to broaden the channel for the flow of their surplus wealth by seeking foreign markets and foreign investments to take off the goods and capital they cannot sell or use at home.

The fallacy of the supposed inevitability of imperial expansion as a necessary outlet for progressive industry is now manifest. It is not industrial progress that demands the opening up of new markets and areas of investment, but mal-distribution of consuming power which prevents the absorption of commodities and capital within the country. The over-saving which is the economic root of Imperialism is found by analysis to consist of rents, monopoly profits, and other unearned or excessive elements of income, which, not being earned by labour of head or hand, have no legitimate *raison d'être*. Having no natural relation to effort of production, they impel their recipients to no corresponding satisfaction of consumption: they form a surplus wealth, which, having no proper place in the normal economy of production and consumption, tends to accumulate as excessive savings. Let any turn in the tide of politico-economic forces divert from these owners their excess of income and make it flow, either to the workers in higher wages, or to the community in taxes, so that it will be spent instead of being saved, serving in either of these ways to swell the tide of consumption –

there will be no need to fight for foreign markets or foreign areas of investment.

(*Imperialism*, Nisbet, 1903, pp. 85–91)

I.6 French Ministry of Finances, table of incomes by category (1894–95)

The table of incomes by categories inserted by Doumer in his draft tax on incomes in 1894–5 gives the following figures established by an extra-parliamentary commission:

Category of income in Francs	No. of incomes by category	Total of incomes by category
2,500 and less	9,509,800	12,342,000,000
2,501 to 3,000	563,000	1,597,000,000
3,001 to 5,000	446,000	1,735,000,000
5,001 to 10,000	294,000	2,109,000,000
10,001 to 20,000	123,400	1,898,000,000
20,001 to 50,000	51,000	1,573,000,000
50,001 to 100,000	9,800	674,000,000
100,001 and more	3,000	572,000,000
Total	11,000,000	225,000,000,000

(E. Levasseur, *Questions ouvrières et industrielles en France sous la IIIe République*, Paris, Arthur Rousseau, 1907, p. 619; trans. A. Marwick)

I.7 Jules Bertaut, from *What the French Provinces Were Like Before the War* (1918)

Chance allowed me, several months before the war, to return to spend several weeks in the provincial town where I passed my very first years. That town is Clarmonde, capital of the department of Basse-Indre . . . Here I have now put together the notes taken at that time.

CONTENTS

12

I

Clarmonde is a medium-sized town, a prefecture of 42,847 inhabitants
. . . It is a small French town which has remained almost unchanged
throughout the last century. . . .

II

M. Pellegrin is the son of a very fine Clarmonde doctor who, for more than
forty years, carried out his duties in my little town and gathered together a
pretty fortune. When his son reached the age of choosing a job for
himself, he naturally opted for the law, as people do who have no settled
ideas about their fortune. He went to Paris, got to know the Latin quarter,
lived it up there in moderate fashion as befitted a good son of the family,
acquitted himself well in his voluntary service in the cavalry and found
himself, approaching his twenty-fifth birthday, ready to join the bar at
Clarmonde and to get married. He married the daughter of a barrister,
Mlle Simonnet . . . The law courts never interested him, save as a source
of income, and from then on his sights were set higher, on the nobility
itself.

To get that far was a hard climb for the son of a simple Clarmonde
doctor. It required twenty years of diplomacy from M. Pellegrin-
Simonnet, but today he can say with satisfaction that he made it: he
receives at table the finest flowers of the Clarmonde nobility, is invited to
the best hunts in the locality, and has been admitted, for seven or eight
years, as a member of the Artistic and Literary Circle of Clarmonde, the
magic formula alone capable of opening the door to every salon.

Yes, truly, M. Pellegrin-Simonnet has arrived, which is no more than
just, for this grand bourgeois, son and grandson of excellent bourgeois,
presents, at bottom, the same qualities, displays the same faults, is
inspired by the same spirit and adopts the same manners as the aristocracy. However, there are slight differences, and it is not at all necessary to
be a highly subtle observer to pick them out. In vain for M. Pellegrin-
Simonnet to invite my good friend the Marquis of Rocquemart or receive
at his table the Baron Jampy: it is very clear that his outlook differs
somewhat from theirs.

III

M. de Geneville has been a widower for a dozen years and has divided his time between the education of his children and the Archaeological Society of Clarmonde, in which he is actively involved. His fortune is modest, twenty thousand pounds in rents, I am told, but sufficient for him to maintain his status. The winter is spent here, and the summer in a small property in the countryside. Only two servants. The well organized household is maintained with perfect care. This man has an innate taste, an almost feminine taste for everything concerning the arrangement of the décor; he has made of his house something exquisite and, above all, French. . . .

Something this week gave me great pleasure: I became a temporary member of the Artistic and Literary Circle of Clarmonde. Note that I am only a temporary member. Nonetheless it was a great favour granted by M. Pellegrin-Simonnet, for the Artistic and Literary Circle of Clarmonde is, as everyone knows, the most exclusive of the town and indeed of the region . . . Belonging to the Circle here is equivalent to being a member of the Jockey Club in Paris. . . .

VII

One of the greatest revolutions in Clarmonde of the last few years is the privilege granted to young women to go out unaccompanied. Strangely, the fashion was launched by the aristocracy itself. It sufficed that there were half a dozen society ladies who, having reached the age of thirty-five without finding suitors, decided to break the rules of public modesty and began this new way of life. Today it is accepted and everyone finds this new-won liberty natural. . . .

XI

It would be to know little of my small town to know only the aristocratic classes and the functionaries. The juice, the pith of Clarmonde, if I may put it thus, is provided by the bourgeoisie, the petty bourgeoisie bordering the people but never mixing with them, the middle bourgeoisie comprising above all the shop-keepers, but most important the independent bourgeoisie holding land or house, the bourgeoisie rooted to the soil of Clarmonde for generations. . . .

One of the most striking features of Clarmonde is the number of young people one meets who have already retired.

Is it that their fortunes are so great and have been won at such great speed in local business? Not at all . . . the real extent of the resources of these petty bourgeois is astonishingly small. From which one must conclude that my fellow citizens prefer a mediocre life without stress to striving feverishly for a well-rewarded one. . . .

XIV

Wanderers are not confined to the superior variety. My little town includes also people much less celebrated . . . who form the vast battalion of the petty functionaries.

They are a well-organized proletariat, situated at the crossroads of the petty bourgeoisie, the people, and the grand functionaries, which, through this strategic position, commands all routes.

Direct issue of the people, it knows all the pathways in this vast country . . . Neighbour of the petty bourgeoisie, it has been influenced by the same selfishness, harder than that of the peasant: it has acquired the spirit of avarice and the taste for money. . . .

XV

Baron Jampy, as everyone knows, is a big man in Paris, but at Clarmonde, in society, Baron Jampy is more than a big man, he is a sort of god. For the ruined petty aristocracy, for the grand aristocracy busy ruining itself, for the high bourgeoisie enraged at not being able to ruin itself through joining the nobility, Baron Jampy appears in the manner of one of these high and mighty lords of the Middle Ages with powers of life and death over an entire region. . . .

XVI

One of the liveliest memories of my childhood is of the passionate interest my family took in local political struggles, with the name which was most frequently mentioned in connection with meetings, addresses, or elections, being one which at once struck me by its popular sound, being that of Barouille. . . .

To say it all in a word, Barouille is a radical-socialist. . . .

In addition, Barouille appears as a sound and honest bourgeois, a tailor by profession, who lives with his wife and daughter in a modest shop. . . . He has a kind of citizenly dignity which he calls 'respect for each individual' and which quite simply is the bourgeois pride which has always kept him from associating with the riff-raff or hanging around in bars. . . .

(*Ce qu'était la province française avant la guerre*, Paris, La Renaissance du Livre, 1918; trans. A. Marwick)

I.8 Leon and Maurice Bonneff, from *The Tragic Life of the Workers* (1908)

THE IRON WORKERS

The Age of Steel is the name which History will no doubt give our epoch. There is scarcely a building in which steel or iron does not occupy an important place, often the most important. They are replacing wood in the framework of buildings; they are eliminating stone in the construction of bridges; soon even steel will have established its place on the streets of cities: experimental steel paving in 'worn out' streets has given good results. In 1903 world production of steel reached 49,902,079 metric tonnes.

To tear the crude metal out of the soil, to smelt it and render it suitable for industrial manufacture, thousands of workers have risked their lives.

The operations of the large-scale metallurgical industries, together with the smaller metal works, require a force of 563,830 male and female workers. In 1906, 93,688 of these workers (perhaps nearly *twenty per cent*) were victims, in the course of their work, of accidents of varying seriousness, but which all involved an absence from work of more than four days.

277 were killed outright.

4,518 were crippled for the rest of their lives, limbs crushed, eyes burned. Women, girls, boys of sixteen were struck down.

The detailed table of accidents happening in one year (1905) provides the evidence:

	Employed	Injured
The large-scale metallurgical industries		
Boys under 18	6,969	2,406 or 34.2%
Girls under 18	77	5 or 6.7%
Girls and women over 18	6,532	6 or 3.6%
Adult males	77,751	19,564 or 25.1%
Smaller metal works		
Boys under 18	59,006	7,108 or 12.0%
Girls under 18	7,131	345 or 4.8%
Women	24,581	953 or 3.8%
Adult males	387,662	46,390 or 11.8%

The number of accidents shows a steady rise from year to year:

Year	Accidents
1903	58,705
1904	63,154
1905	76,797

And already it is clear that this last total will be exceeded in 1906.

Few jobs demand such an effort under such hot temperatures as those of the metal workers; few are accompanied by such a wide range of dangers.

(*La vie tragique des travailleurs: enquêtes sur la condition économique et morale des ouvriers et ouvrières d'industrie*, preface by Lucien Descartes, Paris, Publications Jules Rouff et cie, 1908, pp. 74–6; trans. A. Marwick)

I.9 André Lainé, from *The Shop Girls of Paris* (1911)

'Paris is the paradise of women', states an old proverb. This proverb, though, alas, like many others, quite untrue, nonetheless has wide currency. From far-off sub-prefectures, from the chief villages of un-known cantons, every year more than 10,000 women arrive in this promised paradise which always has in store for them material – and often moral – destitution.

The rich woman finds in Paris the means of satisfying every caprice; the female worker there, more than anywhere else, is subject to utter exploitation.

The moral destitution of the shop girls has seemed to us most distress-ing – infinitely more distressing than their material destitution. A woman, as everyone knows, rarely earns enough to live on. It has to be said that in every sort of work it always turns out that the woman's wage falls *a little below* what is indispensable for subsistence: must she make up the difference through reminding herself she is female and that a daughter of the people has only one means of existence – prostitution?

The question, posed like that, is too serious and too general for us to dare respond in the affirmative. All that we can say, and we believe that we have given abundant proof, is that the wages of the majority of shop girls does not enable them to make ends meet. They have to have recourse to 'someone who provides help'. Usually it is a father or husband, but not everyone has a father who is in a position to support them.

These must 'take a friend'. The owners know this; it is even they who offer the advice. 'I know of no more horrible proof of male egotism, supported by social convention', reports the Countess of Villermont, referring to the reply of a director of a large Paris store which I shall now cite. On certain days and at certain times he interviews women seeking work, perhaps as counter assistants or as cashiers, in his shops. He only poses one brutal question: 'Do you have a protector?' And if the poor creature, blushing or offended, says 'no', he turns his back on her and turns to the next applicant, saying: 'In that case, Mademoiselle, it's impossible to take you on, our wages are too small to keep you alive and we don't want people who look miserable or who are dying of hunger. When you have chosen a friend, you may come back.'

(*Les demoiselles de magasin à Paris*, Paris, 1911; trans. A. Marwick)

I.10 Dr Professor E. Noseda, 'Social insurance' (1913)

A. OPTIONAL INSURANCE

Title I
Constitution and administration of the fund

1 There is instituted a national benevolent fund for the incapacity or old age of workers. This constitutes an autonomous corporation, with its

central office in Rome, and with secondary, departmental, provincial or communal offices, according to the rules set out in the governing statute of the fund, approved by royal decree and passed by the Council of Social Insurance and the Council of State.

As an autonomous body the said national benevolent fund has an agency and its own administration, distinct from that of the State, which is prohibited from taking on any other responsibilities or duties outside what is laid down in the following articles.

Title IV

Joining the Fund

13 Those who may join the national benevolent fund are Italian citizens of both sexes who render service of work by the day or who in general do work which is predominantly manual for third parties or also on their own account, provided that, in this latter case, they do not pay, in whatever form, taxes to the State higher than 30 lire a year.

Married women may join without needing the consent of their husband, and minors without the authorization of whoever exercises the paternal authority or guardianship. . . .

(*Manuale di legislazione sociale italiana*, Milan, 1913; trans. A. Marwick)

I.11 Adelheid Popp, from *The Autobiography of a Working Woman* (1912)

PREFACE TO THE THIRD EDITION BY THE AUTHOR

I have to thank Auguste Bebel most heartily for undertaking the responsibility of publishing the story of my youth. . . . I have mentioned my all too short married life, not in order to speak about myself, but to show by my individual experience that the public activity of a woman must not be hampered by her marriage and duties as wife and mother. This is connected with one of the greatest problems of the woman's question, one of the most important preliminaries in the discussion as to the qualifications of women for perfect political and social equality with men.

FROM THE AUTOBIOGRAPHY

. . . At an age when others are enjoying all the blessedness of childhood, I had already forgotten childish laughter, and was thoroughly imbued with the feeling that work was my destined lot.

The burden of this childhood influenced my disposition for a long time, and made me a creature disliking mirth from my earliest years. Much had to happen, something great had to step into my life to help me to conquer.

♦   ♦   ♦

I found work again; I took everything that was offered me in order to show my willingness to work, and I passed through much. But at last things became better. I was recommended to a great factory which stood in the best repute. Three hundred girls and about fifty men were employed. I was put in a big room where sixty women and girls were at work. Against the windows stood twelve tables, and at each sat four girls. We had to sort the goods which had been manufactured, others had to count them, and a third had to brand on them the mark of the firm. We worked from 7 a.m. to 7 p.m. We had an hour's rest at noon, half-an-hour in the afternoon. Although there was a holiday in the week in which I began work, I received the full wages paid to beginners. That was four florins. I had never yet been paid so much. Besides that, the prospect was held out to me after a few months' steady application, of receiving an increase of a shilling. I received it in six weeks' time, and in six months I was earning ten shillings; later I received twelve shillings.

I seemed to myself to be almost rich. I reckoned how much I could save in the course of a year, and built castles in the air. As I had been accustomed to extraordinary privation, I should have considered it extravagant to spend more now on my food. If I only did not feel hungry, I never even considered of what my food consisted. I only wanted to be well dressed, so that if I went to church on Sunday no one should guess I was a factory worker. For I was ashamed of my work. Working in a factory had always seemed to me to be degrading. When I was an apprentice I had always heard it said that factory girls were bad, disorderly, and depraved. They were always talked about in the most scornful manner, and I had also adopted this false notion. Now I myself was going to a factory where there were so many girls. . . .

◆ ◆ ◆

I had no notion yet of the 'Woman Question'. There was nothing about it in my newspaper, and now I only read Social Democratic publications. I was held to be an exception, and I looked upon myself as such. I considered the social question, as far as I then understood it, as a man's question just like politics. Only I would have liked to be a man, to have a right to bury myself with politics. I only heard for the first time that Social Democrats wanted to procure for women equal political rights with men when, after the Congress at Hainfeld of the Austrian Social Democratic Labour Party, I read the Social Democratic Programme. But I still did not know how women themselves might share in the work of the party.

◆ ◆ ◆

. . . When I had to go away some days to meetings, I often entreated: 'Do say for once that you do not want me to leave you alone with the children, then I shall find it easier to draw back.' But he answered in his simple goodness: 'For my own sake and for that of the children I should wish you to stay here; but as a member of the party, I wish that you should not draw back from performing your duty.' . . . In spite of the heavy burden of work and the great responsibility he had to bear, he forced himself to save time to look after the children and watch over their health. Therefore I always understood how heavy public work is for a mother, because I know what a sacrifice it entails. What has not my husband gone without to make such work possible for his wife – work which he considered useful to the working classes. . . .

Once when I came home from a long propaganda journey which I had undertaken at his express wish, I found him so ill that I immediately fetched the doctor. . . .

. . . he did so share the happiness of living to see that for which he was daily ready to sacrifice his life – the growing greatness and power of the working classes.

♦ ♦ ♦

When I felt the necessity of writing how I became a Socialist, it was solely with the wish of encouraging those numerous working women who possess hearts full of a longing desire to do something, but who always draw back again, because they do not trust their own capabilities. Socialism could change and strengthen others, as it did me. The more consciously I became a Socialist, the more free and strong I felt to meet all opponents. My belief in Socialism had become strong as a rock, and I was never tempted for a moment to waver from it.

When, after my marriage, I was once imprisoned on account of a critique on the present institution of marriage, I never for a moment thought of repentance as I sat lonely in my bare cell. On the contrary, when in the twilight I walked up and down my solitary cell, which I could pace with fourteen steps, I meditated on how I could make up for my lost time. I worked at educating myself further in Socialism, and read scientific books, for which I had usually no time. When my husband came to visit me I could not wait to read the party organ which he secretly slipped into my hands. . . .

The goal is wonderfully beautiful; it is so promising that strength can be found to conquer any difficulty in the way. If I have succeeded in helping to this end in my modest work, then I have attained my aim.

(*The Autobiography of a Working Woman*, trans. F. C. Harvey, T. Fisher Unwin, 1912)

I.12 Werner Sombart, from *The Quintessence of Capitalism* (c. 1913)

The German undertaker (together with the American, whom he is approaching very closely) represents today the most perfect type of this species of the human race. He is distinguished from other modern types possibly in the following ways:

(a) *His adaptability*. German dominance in the world-markets owes much to the German's capacity of adapting himself to the wishes and peculiarities of his customers. Numerous observers have noted this fact many a time and oft. The quality is also exercised in his quick understanding of any set of conditions and in accommodating himself to them.

(b) *His great organizing talent*. See what this had done for German shipping, banking, and electrical works. No other nation has it in so great a measure, not even the Americans.

(c) *His attitude to science*. This too is universally admitted – that Germany's great industries, especially the electrical and chemical industries, have become so mighty because of their careful attention to the results of natural science, and the utilization of those results in their methods of production.

The attitude of the German undertaker to economic science is on the point of being determined. For the moment it seems that it is going to be another characteristic of the German undertaker that he will recognize as a condition for success the need to organize his business in accordance with the results of economic teaching. This much can even be asserted now: method in business enterprise, or, in other words, commercial calculations, have reached their most complete form in the German schools for capitalist undertakers.

(*The Quintessence of Capitalism*, trans. M. Epstein, T. Fisher Unwin, 1915)

I.13   John Galsworthy, letters to (a) David Garnett (18 Sept. 1910) and (b) Edward Garnett (15 Nov. 1910)

(a) to David Garnett

. . . I am not so tolerant at heart of the aristocrat as you – because their seeming class qualities of simplicity, consideration, high spirit, and a sort of stoicism, are partly the outcome of life's kindness to them, and partly artificially fostered for their own self-preservation. Scratch them and you will soon find the Squire or bourgeois. . . .

(b) to Edward Garnett

. . . The so-called 'well-bred' man and woman is now a very wide class, and only those who have been through the fashionable public-school and Varsity curriculum as I have (and with an inner eye as mine is) can appreciate the at once levelling and formative power of that system. It has brought aristocracy (who all pass through it now) completely off its perch. I have left out of the enclosed list *nouveau* or *parvenu* aristocracy (except perhaps half-a-dozen); they're nearly all old-stock, but I assure I could parallel them two or three times over with 'well-bred' men and women quite untitled from whom you couldn't tell them. A slight extra regularity of features; an answer to more high spirits; a harder and less receptive turn of mind is common to all this class which has blood in it; but it's by no means confined to titled gents. . . .

(*Letters from John Galsworthy 1900–1932*, ed. Edward Garnett, Jonathan Cape, 1934, pp. 193, 197)

I.14 William Le Queux, from *The Invasion of 1910* (1906)

'THE SURPRISE'

. . . In a moment the superintendent had taken the operator's seat, adjusted the ear-piece, and was in conversation with Ipswich. A second later he was speaking with the man who had actually witnessed the cutting of the trunk line.

While he was thus engaged an operator at the farther end of the switchboard suddenly gave vent to a cry of surprise and disbelief.

'What do you say, Beccles? Repeat it,' he asked excitedly. Then a moment later he shouted aloud:

'Beccles says that German soldiers – hundreds of them – are pouring into the place! The Germans have landed at Lowestoft, they think.'

All who heard these ominous words sprang up dumbfounded, staring at each other.

The assistant-superintendent dashed to the operator's side and seized his apparatus.

'Halloa – halloa, Beccles! Halloa – Halloa – Halloa!'

The response was some gruff words in German, and sounds of scuffling could distinctly be heard. Then all was silent. . . .

But what held everyone breathless in the trunk telephone headquarters was that the Germans had actually effected the surprise landing that had so often been predicted by the military critics; that England on that quiet September Sunday morning had been attacked. England was actually invaded. It was incredible!

(*The Invasion of 1910*, Eveleigh Nash, 1906, ch. 1, pp. 9–10)

I.15 Friedrich Bernhardi, from *Germany and the Next War* (1912)

The openly declared aims of England and France are the more worthy of attention since an *entente* prevails between the two countries. In the face of these claims the German nation, from the standpoint of its importance to civilization, is fully entitled not only to demand a place in the sun, as Prince Bulow used modestly to express it, but to aspire to an adequate share in the sovereignty of the world far beyond the limits of its present sphere of influence. But we can only reach this goal, by so amply securing our position in Europe, that it can never again be questioned. Then only we need no longer fear that we shall be opposed by stronger opponents whenever we take part in international politics. We shall then be able to exercise our forces freely in fair rivalry with the other world Powers, and secure to German nationality and German spirit throughout the globe that high esteem which is due to them. . . .

We have long underestimated the importance of colonies. Colonial possessions which merely serve the purpose of acquiring wealth, and are only used for economic ends, while the owner-State does not think of colonizing in any form of raising the position of the aboriginal population in the economic or social scale, are unjustifiable and immoral, and can never be held permanently. . . .

We are already suffering severely from the want of colonies to meet our requirements. They would not merely guarantee a livelihood to our growing working population, but would supply raw materials and food-stuffs, would buy goods, and open a field of activity to that immense capital of intellectual labour forces which is today unproductive in Germany, or is in the service of foreign interests. We find throughout the countries of the world German merchants, engineers, and men of every profession, employed actively in the service of foreign masters, because German colonies, when they might be profitably engaged, do not exist. In the future, however, the importance of Germany will depend on two points: firstly, how many millions of men in the world speak German? Secondly, how many of them are politically members of the German Empire?

(*Germany and the Next War*, trans. Allen H. Powles, Edward Arnold, 1912)

I.16 Rachael Low, Appendix B to Ch. 1, from *The History of the British Film 1906–1914* (1949)

Towns with population of 100,000 or over	Population	Picture theatres
Aberdeen	163,891	20
Belfast	315,492	30
Birkenhead	130,794	18
Birmingham	525,833	48
Blackburn	133,052	10
Bolton	180,851	16
Bradford	235,436	31
Brighton	131,237	18
Bristol	357,048	33
Burnley	106,322	9
Cardiff	182,259	21
Coventry	106,349	8
Croydon	169,551	12
Derby	123,410	9
Dublin	309,272	13
Dundee	165,004	6
Edinburgh	320,318	38
Gateshead-on-Tyne	116,197	14
Glasgow	784,496	42
Halifax	101,553	11
Huddersfield	107,821	11
Hull	277,991	35
Leeds	445,550	56
Leicester	227,222	14
Liverpool	745,421	33

Towns with population of 100,000 or over	Population	Picture theatres
Manchester	714,333	111
Middlesbrough	104,767	7
Newcastle-on-Tyne	266,603	32
Norwich	121,478	8
Nottingham	259,904	21
Oldham	147,483	14
Plymouth	112,030	12
Portsmouth	231,141	19
Preston, Lancs.	117,088	8
Salford	231,357	17
Sheffield	459,916	34
Southampton	119,012	15
South Shields	108,647	12
Stockport	108,682	13
Sunderland	151,159	27
Swansea	114,663	19

Figures compiled from Kinematograph Year Book, 1915.

On an arithmetical average, each town with a population of over 100,000 had 22 picture theatres.

(*The History of the British Film 1906–1914*, Allen and Unwin, 1949, p. 51)

I.17   Giovanni Giolitti, 'Giolitti assesses his first year in office' (1904)

REPORT OF OCTOBER 18, 1904, REQUESTING THAT THE
KING DISSOLVE THE CHAMBER OF DEPUTIES AND
CALL NEW ELECTIONS

Your Majesty,

On December 1st of last year the Ministry appeared before Parliament with the programme it intended to follow and asked the Chamber of Deputies for an immediate and explicit vote of confidence. Two days later the Chamber of Deputies gave its approval with a majority of 167 votes.

At that time the programme was criticized by many as too vast and too full of promises. We are pleased to note that after less than a year all the promises that lay within the government's power to fulfil have been kept and that the activity of the legislature developed even more rapidly than was indicated in our programme.

In six months of parliamentary activity we have approved in normal fashion all the budgets of the state and, in addition to a great number of laws of secondary importance, also the following: laws providing for the economic transformation of the region of Basilicata, for the economic and industrial revival of Naples, for the transformation of communal debts in the continental portions of the South, and for the prompt construction of the aqueduct in Apulia. In addition, Parliament approved a radical revision of the law on charitable institutions for the purpose of safeguarding the patrimony of the poor and its allocation to purposes in keeping with the times. It revised the law on public health by intensifying efforts at curing malaria and pellagra and by asserting for the first time the duty of employers to provide better housing conditions for land workers. Measures were taken on behalf of elementary education and elementary schoolteachers with a generosity unknown in all previous legislation, the state contributing 8 million lire a year. The right to compete for public-works contracts was extended to co-operative and agrarian societies. The executive power was deprived of the right to alter the rolls of permanent employees in public administration, and this right was reserved to the legislative power. Many millions were spent for the great improvement of the conditions of the permanent employees in the postal and telegraphic services, in the services of the Finance, Treasury, Foreign Affairs, and Public Works ministries, as well as for the personnel of the state libraries, the judiciary, the prison system, and the junior ranks of the army. A social insurance fund was established for communal employees; the Fund for Workers' Disability and Old Age Pensions was strengthened; pensions were established for workers in the state tobacco monopoly; and provisions were made for the veterans of the wars of independence and for the survivors of Mentana. Measures were taken for putting the finances of the City of Rome on a sound basis, and we kept the old promise of connecting the Trastevere and Termini railroad stations [in Rome]. By means of two agreements with France we provided for the protection of our workers in that country and for the construction of the Cunco-Ventimiglia-Nice railway line. We established a rational four-year plan of public works; we introduced in our penal legislation the sound principle of suspended sentence, and we began a radical reform of the prison system by introducing work in the open and by transforming reformatories from places of punishment into places of education and rehabilitation. Finally, in relation to commercial treaties we took steps to eliminate fraud in the production and sale of wines, to favour the expansion of the wine and citrus fruits industries, to regulate coastal shipping, to improve the fishing industry and the conditions of fishermen, and to promote those industries that use salt and alcohol.

If to this enormous legislative effort already completed we add a number of other items, it will readily be seen how baseless is the accusation made against us (at times with the utmost levity) to the effect that the government has been lacking in effective action for reform. We have negotiated commercial treaties with Germany, Switzerland, and Austria-Hungary and are well along the way in our negotiations with Russia. We have converted the 4.5 per cent rent to 3.5 per cent; we have converted the Roman municipal debt; and we have introduced new and rigid practices in the auditing of state accounts. The absolute necessity of these practices is proved every day by the very fact of the abuses they eliminate. Finally, we have presented a bill that establishes the guidelines for the state's management of those railways which are removed from private management. . . .

These last few years have proved that a regime of freedom benefits the workers more than any other class and that from this regime they have gained very great material and moral benefits. The Ministry is convinced that true prosperity and social peace can be had only by advancing the well-being of the lower classes. Accordingly, it will keep its policy unchanged, trusting that the working classes will have a sufficiently clear understanding of their true interests and of their dignity so as not to allow themselves to be oppressed by selfish tyrannies which spring from below.

This programme of maximum freedom is opposed strenuously by the extreme parties; but the government is determined to remain faithful to it because it has unlimited confidence in the good sense of the Italian people, to whom history has taught that in demagoguery and in reaction it has two equally dangerous enemies. . . .

Italy has entered a new period in its economic and political life . . . It is an essential duty of the government to support this progressive movement by identifying and co-ordinating all of the country's energies. Thus, under the auspices of those institutions which gave us the unity of the fatherland, independence from the foreigner, and maximum freedom, Italy will achieve social peace and that highest degree of civilization, prosperity, and greatness which all those who love the fatherland desire.

It is with these aims in mind that we submit for your signature the decree dissolving the Chamber of Deputies and convening the voters for the coming November 6th, and for the 13th in those constituencies where a second ballot may be necessary.

(Clough, S. B. and Saladine, S. (eds) *A History of Modern Italy: Documents, Reading and Commentary*, New York, Columbia University Press, 1968, pp. 271–3)

I.18 'The Fundamental Laws of Imperial Russia, 1906'

1. The Russian state is unified and indivisible.

2. The Grand Duchy of Finland, while comprising an inseparable part of the Russian state, is governed in its internal affairs by special decrees based on special legislation.

3. The Russian language is the official state language and its use is obligatory in the Army, the Fleet, and in all state and public institutions. The use of local languages and dialects in state and public institutions is determined by special laws.

CHAPTER I. THE ESSENCE OF THE SUPREME
AUTOCRATIC POWER

4. The All-Russian Emperor possesses the supreme autocratic power. Not only fear and conscience, but God himself, commands obedience to his authority.

5. The person of the Sovereign Emperor is sacred and inviolable.

6. The same supreme autocratic power belongs to the Sovereign Empress, should the order of succession to the throne pass to a female line; her husband, however, is not considered a sovereign; except for the title, he enjoys the same honours and privileges reserved for the spouses of all other sovereigns.

7. The Sovereign Emperor exercises the legislative authority jointly with the State Council and the State *Duma*.

8. The Sovereign Emperor enjoys the legislative initiative in all legislative matters. The State Council and the State *Duma* may examine the Fundamental State Laws only on his initiative.

9. The Sovereign Emperor approves laws; and without his approval no legislative measure can become law.

10. The Sovereign Emperor possesses the administrative power in its totality throughout the entire Russian state. On the highest level of administration his authority is direct; on subordinate levels of administration, in conformity with the law, he determines the degree of authority of subordinate branches and officials who act in his name and in accordance with his orders.

11. As supreme administrator, the Sovereign Emperor, in conformity with the existing laws, issues decrees for the organization and functioning of diverse branches of state administration as well as directives essential for the execution of the laws.

12. The Sovereign Emperor alone is the supreme leader of all foreign relations of the Russian state with foreign countries. He also determines the direction of foreign policy of the Russian state.

13. The Sovereign Emperor alone declares war, concludes peace and negotiates treaties with foreign states.

14. The Sovereign Emperor is the Commander-in-Chief of the Russian Army and of the Fleet. He possesses supreme command over all the land and sea forces of the Russian state. He determines the organization of the Army and of the Fleet, and issues decrees and directives dealing with the distribution of the armed forces, their transfer to a war footing, their training, the duration of service by various ranks of the Army and of the Fleet and all other matters related to the organization of the armed forces and the defence of the Russian state. As supreme administrator, the Sovereign Emperor determines limitation on the rights of residence and the acquisition of immovable property in localities that have fortifications and defensive positions for the Army and the Fleet.

15. The Sovereign Emperor has the power to declare martial law or a state of emergency in localities.

16. The Sovereign Emperor has the right to coin money and to determine its physical appearance.

17. The Sovereign Emperor appoints and dismisses the Chairman of the Council of Ministers, Ministers, and Chief Administrators of various departments, as well as other officials whose appointment or dismissal has not been determined by law.

18. As supreme administrator the Sovereign Emperor determines the scope of activity of all state officials in accordance with the needs of the state.

19. The Sovereign Emperor grants titles, medals and other state distinctions as well as property rights. He also determines conditions and procedure for gaining titles, medals, and distinctions.

20. The Sovereign Emperor directly issues decrees and instructions on matters of property that belongs to him as well as on those properties that bear his name and which have traditionally belonged to the ruling Emperor. The latter cannot be bequeathed or divided and are subject to a different form of alienation. These as well as other properties are not subject to levy or collection of taxes.

21. As head of the Imperial Household, the Sovereign Emperor, in accordance with Regulations on the Imperial Family, has the right to issue regulations affecting princely properties. He also determines the composition of the personnel of the Ministry of the Imperial Household, its organization and regulation, as well as the procedure of its administration.

22. Justice is administered in the name of the Sovereign Emperor in courts legally constituted, and its execution is also carried out in the name of His Imperial Majesty.

23. The Sovereign Emperor has the right to pardon the accused, to mitigate the sentence, and even to completely forgive transgressions; including the right to terminate court actions against the guilty and to free them from trial and punishment. Stemming from royal mercy, he also has the right to commute the official penalty and to generally pardon all exceptional cases that are not subject to general laws, provided such actions do not infringe upon civil rights or the legally protected interests of others.

24. Statutes of the *Svod Zakanov* (Vol. I, part 1, 1892 edition) on the order of succession to the throne (Articles 3–17), on the coming of age of the Sovereign Emperor, on government and guardianship (Articles 18–30), on the ascension to the throne and on the oath of allegiance (Articles 31–34 and Appendix V), on the sacred crowning and anointing (Articles 35 and 36), and on the title of His Imperial Majesty and on the State Emblem (Articles 37–39 and Appendix I), and on the faith (Articles 40–46), retain the force of the Fundamental Laws.

25. The Regulation on the Imperial Family (*Svod Zakanov*, Vol. I, part 1, 1892 edition, Articles 82–179 and Appendices II–IV and VI), while retaining the force of the Fundamental Laws, can be changed or amended only

by the Sovereign Emperor personally in accordance with the procedure established by him, provided these changes or amendments of these regulations do not infringe upon general laws or provided they do not call for new expenditures from the treasury.

26. Decrees and commands that are issued directly or indirectly by the Sovereign Emperor as supreme administrator are implemented either by the Chairman of the Council of Ministers, or a subordinate minister, or a department head, and are published by the Governing Senate.

CHAPTER II. RIGHTS AND OBLIGATIONS OF
RUSSIAN SUBJECTS

27. Conditions for acquiring rights of Russian citizenship, as well as its loss, are determined by law.

28. The defence of the Throne and of the Fatherland is a sacred obligation of every Russian subject. The male population, irrespective of social status, is subject to military service determined by law.

29. Russian subjects are obliged to pay legally instituted taxes and dues and also to perform other obligations determined by law.

30. No one shall be subjected to persecution for a violation of the law except as prescribed by the law.

31. No one can be detained for investigation otherwise than prescribed by law.

32. No one can be tried and punished other than for criminal acts considered under the existing criminal laws, in force during the perpetration of these acts, provided newly enacted laws do not exclude the perpetrated criminal acts from the list of crimes.

33. The dwelling of every individual is inviolable. Breaking into a dwelling without the consent of the owner and search and seizure are allowed only in accordance with the legally instituted procedures.

34. Every Russian subject has the right to freely select his place of dwelling and profession, to accumulate and dispose of property, and to travel abroad without any hindrance. Limits on these rights are determined by special laws.

35. Private property is inviolable. Forcible seizure of immovable property, should state or public need demand such action, is permissible only upon just and decent compensation.

36. Russian subjects have the right to organize meetings that are peaceful, unarmed, and not contrary to the law. The law determines the conditions of meetings, rules governing their termination, as well as limitations on places of meetings.

37. Within the limits determined by law everyone can express his thoughts orally or in writing, as well as distribute these thoughts through publication or other means.

38. Russian subjects have the right to organize societies and unions for purposes not contrary to the law. Conditions for organization of societies and unions, their activity, terms and rules for acquiring legal rights as well as closing of societies and unions, is determined by law.

39. Russian subjects enjoy freedom of religion. Terms to enjoy this freedom are determined by law.

40. Foreigners living in Russia enjoy the rights of Russian subjects, with limitations established by law.

41. Exceptions to the rules outlined in this chapter include localities where martial law is declared or where there exist exceptional conditions that are determined by special laws.

CHAPTER III. LAWS

42. The Russian Empire is governed by firmly established laws that have been properly enacted.

43. Laws are obligatory, without exception, for all Russian subjects and foreigners living within the Russian state.

44. No new law can be enacted without the approval of the State Council and the State *Duma*, and it shall not be legally binding without the approval of the Sovereign Emperor.

45. Should extraordinary circumstances demand, when the State *Duma* is not in session, and the introduction of a measure requires a properly constituted legal procedure, the Council of Ministers will submit such a measure directly to the Sovereign Emperor. Such a measure cannot, however, introduce any changes into the Fundamental Laws, or to the organization of the State Council or the State *Duma*, or to the rules governing elections to the Council or to the *Duma*. The validity of such a measure is terminated if the responsible minister or the head of a special department fails to introduce appropriate legislation in the State *Duma* during the first two months of its session upon reconvening, or if the State *Duma* or the State Council should refuse to enact it into law.

46. Laws issued especially for certain localities or segments of the population are not made void by a new law unless such a voiding is specifically intended.

47. Every law is valid for the future, except in those cases where the law itself stipulates that its force is retroactive or where it states that its intent is to reaffirm or explain the meaning of a previous law.

48. The Governing Senate is the general depository of laws. Consequently, all laws should be deposited in the Governing Senate in the original or in duly authorized lists.

49. Laws are published for general knowledge by the Governing Senate according to established rules and are not legally binding before their publication.

50. Legal decrees are not subject to publication if they were issued in accordance with the rules of the Fundamental Laws.

51. Upon publication, the law is legally binding from the time stipulated by the law itself, or, in the case that such a time is omitted, from the day on which the Senate edition containing the published law is received locally. The law itself may stipulate that telegraph or other media of communication be used to transmit it for execution before its publication.

52. The law cannot be repealed otherwise than by another law. Consequently, until a new law repeals the existing law, the old law retains fully its force.

53. No one can be excused for ignorance of the law once it is duly published.

54. Regulations governing combat, technical, and supply branches of the Armed Forces, as well as rules and orders to institutions and authorized personnel of the military and naval establishments are, as a rule, submitted directly to the Sovereign Emperor upon review by the Military and Admiralty Councils, provided that these regulations, rules, and orders affect primarily the above-mentioned establishments, do not touch on matters of general laws, and do not call for new expenditures from the treasury; or, if they call for new expenditure, are covered by expected savings by the Military or Naval Ministries. In cases where the expected saving is insufficient to cover the projected expenditure, submission of such regulations, rules, and orders for the Emperor's approval is permitted only upon first requesting, in a prescribed manner, the necessary appropriation.

55. Regulations governing military and naval courts are issued in accordance with Regulations on Military and Naval Codes.

CHAPTER IV. THE STATE COUNCIL, STATE *DUMA*, AND THE SCOPE OF THEIR ACTIVITY

56. The Sovereign Emperor, by a decree, annually convenes the session of the State Council and of the State *Duma*.

57. The Sovereign Emperor determines by a decree the length of the annual session of the State Council and of the State *Duma*, as well as the interval between the sessions.

58. The State Council is composed of members appointed by His Majesty and of elected members. The total number of appointed members of the Council called by the Emperor to deliberate in the Council's proceedings cannot exceed the total number of the elected members of the Council.

59. The State *Duma* consists of members elected by the population of the Russian Empire for a period of five years, on the basis of rules governing elections to the *Duma*.

60. The State Council examines the credentials of its members. Equally, the State *Duma* examines the credentials of its members.

61. The same person cannot serve simultaneously as a member of the State Council and as a member of the State *Duma*.

62. The Sovereign Emperor, by a decree, can replace the elected membership of the State Council with new members before its tenure expires. The same decree sets new elections of members of the State Council.

63. The Sovereign Emperor, by a decree, can dissolve the State *Duma* and release its members from their five-year tenure. The same decree must designate new elections to the State *Duma* and the time of its first session.

64. The State Council and the State *Duma* have equal rights in legislative matters.

65. The State Council and the State *Duma* enjoy the constitutional right to submit proposals to repeal or to amend the existing laws as well as to issue new laws, except the Fundamental Law whose review belongs exclusively to the Sovereign Emperor.

66. The State Council and the State *Duma* have a constitutional right to address questions to Ministers and heads of various departments, who legally are under the jurisdiction of the Governing Senate, on matters that stem from violations of laws by them or by their subordinates.

67. The jurisdiction of the State Council and of the State *Duma* includes those matters that are listed in the Rules of the Council and of the *Duma*.

68. Those legislative measures that are considered and approved by the State *Duma* are then submitted to the State Council for its approval. Those legislative measures that have been initiated by the State Council are reviewed by the Council and, upon approval, are submitted to the *Duma*.

69. Legislative measures that have been rejected either by the State Council or by the State *Duma* are considered defeated.

70. Those legislative measures that have been initiated either by the State Council or by the State *Duma* [and approved by both], but which have failed to gain Imperial approval, cannot be re-submitted for legislative consideration during the same session. Those legislative measures that have been initiated by either the State Council or by the State *Duma* and are rejected by either one of the Chambers, can be resubmitted for legislative consideration during the same session, provided the Emperor agrees to it.

71. Legislative measures that have been initiated in and approved by the State *Duma* and then by the State Council, equally as the legislative measures initiated and approved by the State Council and then by the State *Duma*, are submitted by the Chairman of the State Council to the Sovereign Emperor.

72. Deliberations on the state budget [by the State Council and/or by the

State *Duma*] cannot exclude or reduce the set sums for the payment of state debts or other obligations assumed by the Russian state.

73. Revenues, for the maintenance of the Ministry of the Imperial Household, including institutions under its jurisdiction that do not exceed the allocated sum of the state budget for 1906, are not subject to review by either the State Council or the State *Duma*. Equally not subject to review are such changes in specific revenues as stem from decisions based on Regulations of the Imperial Family that have resulted from internal reorganizations.

74. If the state budget is not appropriated before the appropriation deadline, the budget that had been duly approved in the preceding year will remain in force with only such changes as have resulted from those legislative measures that became laws after the budget was approved. Prior to publication of the new budget, on the decision of the Council of Ministers and rulings of Ministries and Special Departments, necessary funds will be gradually released. These funds will not exceed in their totality during any month, however, one-twelfth of the entire budgetary expenditures.

75. Extraordinary budgetary expenditures for war-time needs and for special preparations preceding a war are unveiled in all departments in accordance with existing law on the decision of highest administration.

76. State loans to cover both the estimated and non-estimated expenditures are contracted according to the system established to determine state budgetary revenues and expenditures. State loans to cover expenditures in cases foreseen in Article 74, as well as loans to cover expenditures stipulated in Article 75, are determined by the Sovereign Emperor as supreme administrator. Time and conditions to contract state loans are determined on the highest level of government.

77. If the State *Duma* fails to act on a proposal submitted to it reasonably in advance on the number of men needed for the Army and the Fleet, and a law on this matter is not ready by May 1, the Sovereign Emperor has the right to issue a decree calling to military service the necessary number of men, but not more than the number called the preceding year.

CHAPTER V. COUNCIL OF MINISTERS, MINISTERS, AND HEADS OF VARIOUS DEPARTMENTS

78. By law, the Council of Ministers is responsible for the direction and co-ordination of activities of Ministers and Heads of various departments on matters affecting legislation as well as the highest state administration.

79. Ministers and Heads of various departments have the right to vote in the State Council and in the State *Duma* only if they are members of these institutions.

80. Binding resolutions, instructions, and decisions issued by the Council of Ministers, and Ministers and Heads of various departments, as well

as by other responsible individuals entitled by law, should not be contrary to existing laws.

81. The Chairman of the Council of Ministers, Ministers, and Heads of various departments, are responsible to the Sovereign Emperor for State administration. Each individual member is responsible for his actions and decisions.

82. For official misconducts in office, the Chairman of the Council of Ministers, Ministers and Heads of various departments are subject to civil and criminal punishment established by law.

(*Imperial Russia, A Source Book 1900–1917*, ed. Basil Dmytryshyn, Hinsdale, Ill., The Dryden Press, 1974, pp. 387–93)

I.19 'Programme of the Russian Social Democratic Workers' Party (Bolsheviks)' (Aug. 1903)

The development of exchange has created such close ties among all the peoples of the civilized world that the great proletarian movement toward emancipation was bound to become – and has long since become – international.

Considering itself one of the detachments of the universal army of the proletariat, Russian social democracy is pursuing the same ultimate goal as that for which the social democrats in other countries are striving. This ultimate goal is determined by the nature of contemporary bourgeois society and by the course of its development. The main characteristic of such a society is production for the market on the basis of capitalist production relations, whereby the largest and most important part of the means of production and exchange of commodities belongs to a numerically small class of people, while the overwhelming majority of the population consists of proletarians and semi-proletarians who, by their economic conditions, are forced either continuously or periodically to sell their labour power; that is, to hire themselves out to the capitalists, and by their toil to create the incomes of the upper classes of society.

The expansion of the capitalist system of production runs parallel to technical progress, which, by increasing the economic importance of large enterprises, tends to eliminate the small independent producers, to convert some of them into proletarians, to reduce the socio-economic role of others and, in some localities, to place them in more or less complete, more or less open, more or less onerous dependence on capital.

Moreover, the same technical progress enables the entrepreneurs to utilize to an ever greater extent woman and child labour in the process of production and exchange of commodities. And since, on the other hand, technical improvements lead to a decrease in the entrepreneur's demand for human labour power, the demand for labour power necessarily lags behind the supply, and there is in consequence greater dependence of hired labour upon capital, and increased exploitation of the former by the latter.

Such a state of affairs in the bourgeois countries, as well as the ever growing competition among those countries on the world market, render the sale of goods which are produced in greater and greater quantities ever more difficult. Over-production, which manifests itself in more or less acute industrial crises – which in turn are followed by more or less protracted periods of industrial stagnation – is the inevitable consequence of the development of the productive forces in bourgeois society. Crises and periods of industrial stagnation, in their turn, tend to impoverish still further the small producers, to increase still further the dependence of hired labour upon capital, and to accelerate still further the relative, and sometimes the absolute, deterioration of the condition of the working class.

Thus, technical progress, signifying increased productivity of labour and the growth of social wealth, becomes in bourgeois society the cause of increased social inequalities, of wider gulfs between the wealthy and the poor, of greater insecurity of existence, of unemployment, and of numerous privations for ever larger and larger masses of toilers.

But together with the growth and development of all these contradictions inherent in bourgeois society, there grows simultaneously dissatisfaction with the present order among the toiling and exploited masses; the number and solidarity of the proletarians increases, and their struggle against the exploiters sharpens. At the same time, technical progress, by concentrating the means of production and exchange, by socializing the process of labour in capitalist enterprises, creates more and more rapidly the material possibility for replacing capitalist production relations by socialist ones; that is, the possibility for social revolution, which is the ultimate aim of all the activities of international social democracy as the class-conscious expression of the proletarian movement.

By replacing private with public ownership of the means of production and exchange, by introducing planned organization in the public process of production so that the well-being and the many-sided development of all members of society may be insured, the social revolution of the proletariat will abolish the division of society into classes and thus emancipate all oppressed humanity, and will terminate all forms of exploitation of one part of society by another.

A necessary condition for this social revolution is the dictatorship of the proletariat; that is, the conquering by the proletariat of such political power as would enable it to crush any resistance offered by the exploiters. In its effort to make the proletariat capable of fulfilling its great historical mission, international social democracy organizes it into an independent political party in opposition to all bourgeois parties, directs all the manifestations of its class struggle, discloses before it the irreconcilable conflict between the interests of the exploiters and those of the exploited, and clarifies for it the historical significance of the imminent social revolution and the conditions necessary for its coming. At the same time, it reveals to the other sections of the toiling and exploited masses the hopelessness of their condition in capitalist society and the need of a social revolution if they wish to be free of the capitalist yoke. The party of the working class, the social democracy, calls upon all strata of the toiling and exploited population to join its ranks insofar as they accept the point of view of the proletariat.

On the road towards their common final goal, which is determined by the prevalence of the capitalist system of production throughout the civilized world, the social democrats of different countries must devote themselves to different immediate tasks – first, because that system is not everywhere developed to the same degree; and second, because in different countries its development takes place in a different socio-political setting.

In Russia, where capitalism has already become the dominant mode of production, there are still preserved numerous vestiges of the old pre-capitalist order, when the toiling masses were serfs of the landowners, the state, or the sovereign. Greatly hampering economic progress, these vestiges interfere with the many-sided development of the class struggle of the proletariat, help to preserve and strengthen the most barbarous forms of exploitation by the state and the propertied classes of the millions of peasants, and thus keep the whole people in darkness and subjection.

The most outstanding among these relics of the past, the mightiest bulwark of all this barbarism, is the tsarist autocracy. By its very nature it is bound to be hostile to any social movement, and cannot but be bitterly opposed to all the aspirations of the proletariat towards freedom.

By reason of the above, the first and immediate task put before itself by the Russian Social Democratic Workers' Party is to overthrow the tsarist autocracy and to replace it with a democratic republic whose constitution would guarantee the following:

1. The sovereignty of the people; that is, the concentration of all supreme state power in the hands of a legislative assembly, consisting of people's representatives, and forming one chamber.

2. Universal, equal, and direct suffrage for all male and female citizens, twenty years old or over, at all elections to the legislative assembly and to the various local organs of self-government; the secret ballot at elections; the right of every voter to be elected to any representative institution; biennial parliaments; salaries to be paid to the people's representatives.

3. Broad local self-government; home rule for all localities where the population is of a special composition and characterized by special conditions of life.

4. Inviolability of person and dwelling.

5. Unlimited freedom of religion, speech, press, assembly, strikes, and unions.

6. Freedom of movement and occupation.

7. Abolition of classes; equal rights for all citizens, irrespective of sex, religion, race, or nationality.

8. The right of any people to receive instruction in its own language, to be secured by creating schools at the expense of the state and the local organs of self-government; the right of every citizen to use his native language at meetings; the introduction of the use of the native language on a par with the state language in all local, public, and state institutions.

9. The right of self-determination for all nations included in the composition of the state.

10. The right of any person to sue any official before a jury in the regular way.

11. Election of judges by the people.

12. Replacement of the standing army by a general armament of the people.

13. Separation of church and state, and of school and church.

14. Free and compulsory general and professional education for all children of both sexes up to the age of sixteen; provision by the state of food, clothing, and school supplies for poor children.

As a basic condition for the democratization of our *state economy* the Russian Social Democratic Workers' Party demands the abolition of all indirect taxes and the establishment of a progressive tax on income and inheritances.

In order to *safeguard the working class* against physical and moral degeneration, as well as to insure the development of its power to carry on the struggle for freedom, the party demands the following:

1. Eight-hour working day for all hired labour.

2. A law providing a weekly uninterrupted forty-two-hour respite for all hired labour, of both sexes, in all branches of the national economy.

3. Complete prohibition of overtime work.

4. Prohibition of night work (from 9 p.m. to 6 a.m.) in all branches of the national economy, with the exception of those in which this is absolutely necessary because of technical considerations approved by labour organizations.

5. Prohibition of the employment of children of school age (up to sixteen) and restriction of the working day of minors (from sixteen to eighteen) to six hours.

6. Prohibition of female labour in those branches of industry which are injurious to women's health; relief from work four weeks before and six weeks after childbirth, with regular wages paid during all this period.

7. Establishment of nurseries for infants and children in all shops, factories, and other enterprises that employ women; permission for

freedom of at least a half-hour's duration to be granted at three-hour intervals to all nursing mothers.

8. Old-age state insurance, and insurance against total or partial disability; such insurance to be based on a special fund formed from a tax levied on the capitalists.

9. Prohibition of payment of wages in kind; establishment of regular weekly pay days when all wages shall be paid in money in absolute conformity with all the agreements relating to the hire of workers; wages to be paid during working hours.

10. Prohibition of deductions by employers from workers' wages, on any ground or for any purpose (fines, spoilage, and so forth).

11. Appointment of an adequate number of factory inspectors in all branches of the national economy and extension of their supervision to all enterprises employing hired labour, including government enterprises (domestic service also to be within the sphere of their supervision); appointment of special women inspectors in those industries where female labour is employed; participation of representatives, elected by the workers and paid by the state, in supervising the enforcement of the factory laws, the fixing of wage scales, and in accepting or rejecting the finished products and other results of labour.

12. Control by organs of local self-government, together with representatives elected by the workers, over sanitation in the dwellings assigned to the workers by the employers, as well as over internal arrangements in those dwellings and the renting conditions – in order to protect the workers against the employers' interference with their life and activity as private citizens.

13. Establishment of properly organized sanitary control over all establishments employing hired labour, the medico-sanitary organization to be entirely independent of the employers; in time of illness, free medical aid to be rendered to the workers at the expense of the employers, with the workers retaining their wages.

14. Establishment of criminal responsibility in the case of employers' infringement upon the laws intended to protect the workers.

15. Establishment in all branches of the national economy of industrial courts to be composed of representatives of workers and employers in equal numbers.

16. Imposition upon the organs of local self-government of the duty of establishing employment agencies (labour exchanges) to deal with the hiring of local and out-of-town labour in all branches of industry, and participation of workers' and employers' representatives in their administration.

In order to *remove the vestiges of serfdom* that fall directly and heavily upon the peasants, and to encourage the free development of the class struggle in the *village*, the party demands above all:

1. Abolition of redemption payments and quit rents as well as all obligations which presently fall on the peasantry, the tax-paying class.

2. Repeal of all laws which restrict the peasant in disposing of his land.

3. Return to peasants of money collected from them in the form of redemption payments and quit rents; confiscation of monastery and church properties as well as property belonging to princes, government agencies, and members of the royal family; imposition of a special tax on lands of nobles who have sold it on loan terms; transfer of the money thus procured into a special reserve fund to meet cultural and charitable needs of villages.

4. Organization of peasant committees: (a) to return to villages (by means of expropriation . . .) those lands which were taken away from the peasants at the emancipation, and which are held by the nobles as a means of enserfment of peasants; (b) to transfer to peasant ownership those lands in the Caucasus which they use now on a temporary basis; (c) to eliminate the remnants of serfdom still in effect in the Urals, the Altai, the Western Provinces, and other parts of the country.

5. Grant to the courts the right to lower unusually high rents and to annul those contracts which contain slave characteristics.

To attain its immediate goals, the Russian Social Democratic Workers' Party will support every opposition and revolutionary movement directed against the existing social and political system in Russia. At the same time it rejects all reformist projects whose aim is to extend or to consolidate bureaucratic-police protection over the toiling classes.

On its own part, the Russian Social Democratic Workers' Party is firmly convinced that a full, consistent, and thorough realization of the indicated political and social changes can only be attained by the overthrow of autocracy and by the convocation of a Constituent Assembly freely elected by the entire people.

(*Imperial Russia, A Source Book 1900–1917*, ed. Basil Dmytryshyn, Hinsdale, Ill., The Dryden Press, 1974, pp. 394–9)

I.20   'Programme of the Russian Constitutional Democratic Party (Kadets)' (1905)

I. BASIC RIGHTS OF CITIZENS

1. All Russian citizens, irrespective of sex, religion, or nationality, are equal before the law. All class distinctions and all limitations of personal and property rights of Poles, Jews, and all other groups of the population, should be repealed.

2. Every citizen is guaranteed freedom of conscience and religion. No persecution for religious beliefs or convictions, or for change or refusal to accept religious indoctrination, can be allowed. The celebration of reli-

gious and church ceremonies and the spread of beliefs is free, provided these activities do not include any general transgressions contrary to the criminal code of law. The Orthodox Church and other religions should be freed from state protection.

3. Anyone who wishes to express his thoughts orally or in writing has the right to publish and spread them through printing or any other media. Censorship, both general and special, regardless of its name, must be abolished and cannot be reinstituted. For their oral or written transgressions the guilty ones will answer before the court.

4. All Russian citizens have the right to organize public or private meetings, in dwellings as well as in the open air, to examine any problem they wish.

5. All Russian citizens have the right to organize unions or societies without needing permission for it.

6. The right to petition is granted to every citizen as well as to all groups, unions, gatherings, and so forth.

7. The person and home of every individual should be inviolable. Entering of a private dwelling, search, seizure, and opening of private correspondence, are allowed only in cases permitted by law or on order of the court. Any individual detained in cities or places where courts are located should be freed within twenty-four hours; in other localities of the Empire not later than three days, or be brought before the court. Any detention undertaken illegally, or without proper grounds, gives a detained person the right to be compensated by the state for losses suffered.

8. No one can be subjected to persecution or punishment except on the basis of law by court authorities in a legally constituted court. No extraordinary courts are allowed.

9. Every citizen has freedom of movement and travel abroad. The passport system is abolished.

10. All the above-mentioned rights of citizens must be incorporated into the Constitution of the Russian Empire and be guaranteed by courts.

11. The Constitution of the Russian Empire should guarantee all the minorities inhabiting the Empire, in addition to full civil and political equality enjoyed by all citizens, the right of cultural self-determination, namely: full freedom of usage of various languages and dialects in public, the freedom to found and maintain educational institutions and meetings of all sorts having as their aim the preservation and development of language, literature and culture of every nationality.

12. Russian language should be the official language of central administration, army, and fleet. The use of local languages alongside the official language in state and public institutions and educational establishments supported by the state or organs of local self-government is determined by general and local laws, and within their competence by the institutions

concerned. The population of each locality should be guaranteed education in the native language in elementary schools, and possibly in subsequent education.

II. GOVERNMENT APPARATUS

13. The constitutional system of the Russian state will be determined by the Constitution.

14. People's representatives are elected by a general, equal, direct and secret ballot, irrespective of their religion, nationality or sex.

The party allows within its midst a difference of opinion on the question of national representation, consisting of one or two chambers, in which case the second chamber should consist of representatives of the local organs of self-government, organized on the basis of a general vote and spread throughout all of Russia.

15. National representation participates in the realization of legislative power, in the determination of government revenues and expenditures, and in control of the legality and expedience of actions of higher and lower organs of administration.

16. No decision, decree, *ukaz*, order or a similar act not based on the legislative measure of national representation, regardless of its name or place of origin, can have the force of law.

17. A government inventory, which should include all revenues and expenditures of the state, should be established by law, every year. No taxes, dues, and collections for the state, as well as state loans, can be established other than by legislation.

18. Members of national representative assemblies should have the right of legislative initiative.

19. Ministers are responsible to the representatives of the national assembly, and the latter have the right of questioning and interpellation.

III. LOCAL SELF-GOVERNMENT AND AUTONOMY

20. Local self-government should be extended throughout the entire Russian state.

21. Representatives in the organs of local self-government, being close to the population by virtue of the organization of small self-governing units, should be elected on the basis of universal, equal, direct, and secret ballot, regardless of sex, religion, and nationality, while the assemblies of higher self-governing units can be selected by lower assemblies. *Gubernia zemstvos* should have the right to enter into temporary or permanent unions among themselves.

22. The competence of the organs of local self-government should include the entire field of local administration, including police, but excluding only those branches of administration which, under the condition of

present state life, must be located in the hands of the central government. Organs of the local self-government should receive partial support from sources which now go to the budget of the central government.

23. The activity of representatives of the central government should be limited to supervision of the legality of acts of the organs of local self-government; the final decision on any disputes or doubts is reserved for the courts.

24. Following the establishment of rights of civil freedom and proper representation with constitutional rights for the entire Russian state, there should be opened a legal way within the framework of state legislation for the establishment of local autonomy and *oblast* representative assemblies, with the right to participate in the realization of legislative authority on familiar matters in accordance with the needs of the population.

25. Immediately following the introduction of the imperial democratic government with constitutional rights, there should be established in the Polish kingdom an autonomous administration with a *sejm* [Parliament] elected on the same basis as the state parliament of Russia, preserving its state unity and participation in the central parliament on an equal footing with other parts of the Empire. Frontiers between the Polish kingdom and neighbouring *gubernias* shall be established in accordance with the native population and desires of the local population. In the Polish kingdom there should be instituted national guarantees of civil freedom and rights of nationalities on cultural self-determination as well as protection of the rights of minorities.

26. *Finland*. The Finnish Constitution, which safeguards its special state status, should be fully reinstated. All future measures common to the Empire and the Grand Duchy of Finland should be solved by an agreement between legislative branches of the Empire and the Grand Duchy.

IV. COURTS

27. All departures from the bases of the Judicial Statute of November 20, 1864, which separated judicial from administrative power (irremovability of judges, independence of courts, and equality of all citizens before the court) as well as the introduction of subsequent novelties are to be abolished . . . Courts with class representatives are abolished. Matters of *volost* justice are subject to the competence of an elected justice of the peace. The *volost* court and the institution of *zemskii nachalniks* [land administrators] are abolished. The demand for property qualifications to perform the functions of a Justice of the Peace as well as that of a sworn deputy is abolished. The principle of the unity of appellate court is re-established. Advocacy is organized on the foundation of true self-administration.

28. In addition to this, the aim of penal policy should consist of:

(a) unconditional abolishment forever of the death penalty; (b) introduction of conditional conviction; (c) establishment of protection during preliminary investigation; and (d) introduction into court proceedings of controvertible rule.

29. The immediate task centres in the full examination of the criminal code, the annulment of decrees which are contrary to the foundations of political freedom, and the reworking of the project of the civil code.

V. FINANCIAL AND ECONOMIC POLICY

30. There should be re-examination of government expenditure in order to eliminate unproductive expenses, and to bring about an appreciable increase of state resources for the real needs of the people.

31. The redemption payments should be repealed.

32. There should be replacement of indirect by direct taxes, general lowering of indirect taxes, and gradual repeal of indirect taxes on items of general consumption.

33. There should be a reform of direct taxes on the basis of progressive income, a reform of property taxation, and a progressive tax on inheritance.

34. In conformity with the condition of individual industries there should be a lowering of custom duties in order to cut down the cost of products of general consumption and to improve the technical level of industry and agriculture.

35. Saving banks should be used for the development of small loans.

VI. AGRARIAN LEGISLATION

36. There should be an increase of arable land for that part of the population which works the land with its own labour, namely landless and petty peasants – as well as other peasants – by state, princely, cabinet, monastery, and private estates at the state's expense, with private owners being compensated at a fair (not market) price for their land.

37. Expropriated land should be transferred to a state and land reserve. Rules by which the land from this reserve should be given to a needy population (ownership, or personal or communal use, and so forth) should be determined in accordance with peculiarities of land ownership and land usage in different parts of Russia.

38. There should be broad organization of government aid to migration, resettlement, and arrangement of the economic life of peasants. There should be reorganization of the Boundary Office, termination of surveying and introduction of other measures for bringing prosperity to the rural population and improving the rural economy.

39. Legislation dealing with the lease relationship should be pro-

mulgated in order to protect the right of tenants and the right to re-lease. . . .

40. The existing rules on hiring of agricultural workers should be repealed and labour legislation should be extended to agricultural workers. . . .

VII. LABOUR LEGISLATION

41. There should be freedom of labour unions and assemblies.

42. The right to strike should be granted. Punishment for violations of law which occur during or as a result of strikes should be determined in general terms and under no circumstances should be extreme.

43. Labour legislation and independent inspection of labour should be extended to all forms of hired labour; there should be participation of workers' elected representatives in inspections aimed at safeguarding the interests of workers.

44. Legislation should introduce the eight-hour working day. Where possible, this norm should be immediately realized everywhere, and systematically introduced in other industries. Night work and overtime work should be prohibited except where technically and socially indispensable.

45. Protection of female and child labour and the establishment of special measures to protect male labour should be developed in dangerous enterprises.

46. Arbitration offices consisting of an equal number of representatives of labour and capital to regulate all kinds of hiring which are not regulated by labour legislation, and solving of disputes which may arise between workers and employers, should be established.

47. Obligatory state medical care (for a definite period), accident and work-connected illness compensations, which are to be contributed to by the employers, should be established.

48. State old age security and disability allowances for all individuals who make a living by their own work should be introduced.

49. Criminal responsibility for violation of laws dealing with the protection of labour should be established.

VIII. PROBLEMS OF EDUCATION

Public education should be founded on freedom, democracy, and decentralization in order to realize the following goals:

50. The elimination of all restrictions on school admissions based on sex, origin or religion.

51. Freedom of private and public initiative to found and organize all sorts of educational institutions, including education outside the school; freedom of instruction.

52. Better liaison should be organized between various school classes in order to make easier a transfer from one school to another.

53. There should be full autonomy and freedom of instruction in universities and other institutions of higher learning. Their numbers should increase. The fee for attending lectures should be lowered. Institutions of higher learning should organize education to meet the needs of broad layers of society. Students should have freedom to organize themselves.

54. The number of institutions of secondary learning should increase in accordance with public needs; the fee for these should be reduced. Local public institutions should have the right to participate in the formulation of the education curriculum.

55. A universal, free, and obligatory system of education should be introduced in elementary schools. Local self-government should extend material aid to those who need it.

56. Local self-government should organize institutions for the education of the adult population – elementary schools for the adult, as well as public libraries and public universities.

57. Professional education should be developed.

(*Imperial Russia, A Source Book 1900–1917*, ed. Basil Dmytryshyn, Hinsdale, Ill., The Dryden Press, 1974, pp. 405–10)

I.21 'The Erfurt programme of the German Social Democratic Party' (1891)

The economic development of bourgeois society leads by natural necessity to the downfall of the small industry, whose foundation is formed by the worker's private ownership of his means of production. It separates the worker from his means of production and converts him into a propertyless proletarian, while the means of production become the monopoly of a relatively small number of capitalists and large landowners.

Hand-in-hand with this monopolization of the means of production goes the displacement of the dispersed small industries by colossal great industries, the development of the tool into the machine, and a gigantic growth in the productivity of human labour. But all the advantages of this transformation are monopolized by capitalists and large landowners. For the proletariat and the declining intermediate classes – petty bourgeoisie and peasants – it means a growing augmentation of the insecurity of their existence, of misery, oppression, enslavement, debasement, and exploitation.

Ever greater grows the number of proletarians, ever more enormous the army of surplus workers, ever sharper the opposition between exploiters and exploited, ever bitterer the class-war between bourgeoisie and proletariat, which divides modern society into two hostile camps, and is the common characteristic of all industrial countries.

The gulf between the propertied and the propertyless is further widened through the crises, founded in the essence of the capitalistic method of production, which constantly become more comprehensive and more devastating, which elevate general insecurity to the normal condition of society, and which prove that the powers of production of contemporary society have grown beyond measure, and that private ownership of the means of production has become incompatible with their intended application and their full development.

Private ownership of the means of production, which was formerly the means of securing to the producer the ownership of his product, has today become the means of expropriating peasants, manual workers, and small traders, and enabling the non-workers – capitalists and large landowners – to own the product of the workers. Only the transformation of capitalistic private ownership of the means of production – the soil, mines, raw materials, tools, machines, and means of transport – into social ownership and the transformation of production of goods for sale into socialistic production managed for and through society, can bring it about, that the great industry and the steadily growing productive capacity of social labour shall for the hitherto exploited classes be changed from a source of misery and oppression to a source of the highest welfare and of all-round harmonious perfection.

The social transformation means the emancipation not only of the proletariat but of the whole human race which suffers under present conditions. But it can only be the work of the working class, because all the other classes, in spite of mutually conflicting interests, take their stand on the basis of private ownership of the means of production, and have as their common object the preservation of the principles of contemporary society.

The battle of the working class against capitalistic exploitation is necessarily a political battle. The working class cannot carry on its economic battles or develop its economic organization without political rights. It cannot effect the passing of the means of production into the ownership of the community without acquiring political power.

To shape this battle of the working class into a conscious and united effort, and to show it its naturally necessary end, is the object of the Social Democratic Party.

The interests of the working class are the same in all lands with capitalistic methods of production. With the expansion of world-transport and production for the world-market, the state of the workers in any one country becomes constantly more dependent on the state of the workers in other countries. The emancipation of the working class is thus a task in which the workers of all civilized countries are concerned in a like degree. Conscious of this, the Social Democratic Party of Germany feels and declares itself *one* with the class-conscious workers of all other lands.

The Social Democratic Party of Germany fights thus not for new class privileges and exceptional rights, but for the abolition of class domination and of the classes themselves, and for the equal rights and equal obligations of all, without distinction of sex and parentage. Setting out from these views, it combats in contemporary society not merely the exploitation and oppression of the wage-workers, but every kind of exploitation and oppression, whether directed against a class, a party, a sex, or a race.

Setting out from these principles the Social Democratic Party of Germany demands immediately:

1. Universal, equal, direct suffrage and franchise, with direct ballot, for all members of the Empire over twenty years of age, without distinction of sex, for all elections and acts of voting. Proportional representation; and until this is introduced, redivision of the constituencies by law according to the numbers of population. A new legislature every two years. Fixing of elections and acts of voting for a legal holiday. Indemnity for the elected representatives. Removal of every curtailment of political rights except in case of tutelage.

2. Direct legislation by the people by means of the initiative and referendum. Self-determination and self-government of the people in empire, state, province, and commune. Authorities to be elected by the people; to be responsible and bound. Taxes to be voted annually.

3. Education of all to be capable of bearing arms. Armed nation instead of standing army. Decision of war and peace by the representatives of the people. Settlement of all international disputes by the method of arbitration.

4. Abolition of all laws which curtail or suppress the free expression of opinion and the right of association and assembly.

5. Abolition of all laws which are prejudicial to women in their relations to men in public or private law.

6. Declaration that religion is a private matter. Abolition of all contributions from public funds to ecclesiastical and religious objects. Ecclesiastical and religious communities are to be treated as private associations, which manage their affairs quite independently.

7. Secularization of education. Compulsory attendance of public primary schools. No charges to be made for instruction, school requisites, and maintenance, in the public primary schools; nor in the higher educational institutions for those students, male and female, who by virtue of their capacities are considered fit for further training.

8. No charge to be made for the administration of the law, or for legal assistance. Judgement by popularly elected judges. Appeal in criminal cases. Indemnification of innocent persons prosecuted, arrested, or condemned. Abolition of the death penalty.

9. No charges to be made for medical attendance, including midwifery and medicine. No charges to be made for death certificates.

10. Graduated taxes on income and property, to meet all public expenses as these are to be covered by taxation. Obligatory self-assessment. A tax on inheritance, graduated according to the size of the inheritance and the degree of kinship. Abolition of all indirect taxes, customs, and other politico-economic measures which sacrifice the interests of the whole community to the interests of a favoured minority.

For the protection of the working class, the German Social Democratic Party demands immediately:

1. An effective national and international legislation for the protection of workmen on the following basis:
(a) Fixing of a normal working day with a maximum of eight hours.
(b) Prohibition of industrial work for children under fourteen years.
(c) Prohibition of night-work, except for such branches of industry as, in accordance with their nature, require night-work, for technical reasons, or reasons of public welfare.
(d) An uninterrupted rest of at least thirty-six hours in every week for every worker.
(e) Prohibition of the truck system.

2. Inspection of all industrial businesses, investigation and regulation of labour relations in town and country by an Imperial Department of Labour, district labour department, and chambers of labour. Thorough industrial hygiene.

3. Legal equalization of agricultural labourers and domestic servants with industrial workers; removal of the special regulations affecting servants.

4. Assurance of the right of combination.

5. Workmen's insurance to be taken over bodily by the Empire; and the workers to have an influential share in its administration.

(German text in *Protokoll über die Verhandlungen des Parteitages der Sozial-demokratischen Partei Deutschlands*, Berlin, 1891; trans. in Vernon Lidtke, *The Outlawed Party: Social Democracy in Germany 1878–1890*, Princeton University Press, 1966, pp. 335–8)

I.22   From The British Old Age Pensions Act (1 Aug. 1908)

1. – (1) Every person in whose case the conditions laid down by this Act for the receipt of an old age pension (in this Act referred to as statutory conditions) are fulfilled, shall be entitled to receive such a pension under this Act so long as those conditions continue to be fulfilled, and so long as he is not disqualified under this Act for the receipt of the pension.

(2) An old age pension under this Act shall be at the rate set forth in the schedule to this Act.

(3) The sums required for the payment of old age pensions under this Act shall be paid out of moneys provided by Parliament.

(4) The receipt of an old age pension under this Act shall not deprive the pensioner of any franchise, right, or privilege, or subject him to any disability.

2. The statutory conditions for the receipt of an old age pension by any person are –

(1) The person must have attained the age of seventy.

(2) The person must satisfy the pension authorities that for at least twenty years up to the date of the receipt of any sum on account of a pension he has been a British subject, and has had his residence, as defined by regulations under this Act, in the United Kingdom.

(3) The person must satisfy the pension authorities that his yearly means as calculated under this Act do not exceed thirty-one pounds ten shillings.

3. – (1) A person shall be disqualified for receiving or continuing to receive an old age pension under this Act, notwithstanding the fulfilment of the statutory conditions –

(a) While he is in receipt of any poor relief (other than relief excepted under this provision). . . .

(b) If, before he becomes entitled to a pension, he has habitually failed to work according to his ability, opportunity, and need, for the maintenance or benefit of himself and those legally dependent upon him:

Provided that a person shall not be disqualified under this paragraph if he has continuously for ten years up to attaining the age of sixty, by means of payments to friendly, provident, or other societies, or trade unions, or other approved steps, made such provision against old age, sickness, infirmity, or want or loss of employment as may be recognised as proper provision for the purpose by regulations under this Act. . . .

(2) Where a person has been before the passing of this Act, or is after the passing of this Act, convicted of any offence, and ordered to be imprisoned without the option of a fine or to suffer any greater punish-

---

SCHEDULE

Means of pensioner	Rate of pension per week	
Where the yearly means of the pensioner as calculated under this Act	*s.*	*d.*
Do not exceed 21*l*	5	0
Exceed 21*l*., but do not exceed 23 *l*. 12*s*. 6*d*.	4	0
Exceed 23*l*. 12*s*. 6*d*., but do not exceed 26*l*. 5*s*.	3	0
Exceed 26*l*. 5*s*., but do not exceed 28*l*. 17*s*. 6*d*.	2	0
Exceed 28*l*. 17*s*. 6*d*., but do not exceed 31*l*. 10*s*.	1	0
Exceed 31*l*. 10*s*.	No pension	

ment, he shall be disqualified for receiving or continuing to receive an old age pension under this Act while he is detained in prison in consequence of the order, and for a further period of ten years after the date on which he is released from prison.

(3) Where a person of sixty years of age or upwards having been convicted before any court is liable to have a detention order made against him under the Inebriates Act, 1898, and is not necessarily, by virtue of the provisions of this Act, disqualified for receiving or continuing to receive an old pension under this Act, the court may, if they think fit, order that the person convicted be so disqualified for such period, not exceeding ten years, as the court direct. . . .

(Old Age Pensions Act, 1908)

I.23 From the British National Insurance Act (16 Dec. 1911)

PART I. NATIONAL HEALTH INSURANCE

Insured Persons
1. – (1) Subject to the provisions of this Act, all persons of the age of sixteen and upwards who are employed within the meaning of this Part of this Act shall be, and any such persons who are not so employed but who possess the qualifications herein-after mentioned may be, insured in manner provided in this Part of this Act, and all persons so insured (in this Act called 'insured persons') shall be entitled in the manner and subject to the conditions provided in this Act to the benefits in respect of health insurance and prevention of sickness conferred by this Part of this Act.

(2) The persons employed within the meaning of this Part of this Act (in this Act referred to as 'employed contributors') shall include all persons of either sex, whether British subjects or not, who are engaged in any of the employments specified in Part I of the First Schedule to this Act, not being employments specified in Part II of that schedule:

Provided that the Insurance Commissioners herein-after constituted may, with the approval of the Treasury, by a special order made in manner herein-after provided, provide for including amongst the persons employed within the meaning of this Part of the Act any persons engaged in any of the excepted employments specified in Part II of the said schedule either unconditionally or subject to such conditions as may be specified in the order.

(3) The persons not employed within the meaning of this Part of this Act who are entitled to be insured persons include all persons who either –

(*a*) are engaged in some regular occupation and are wholly or mainly dependent for their livelihood on the earnings derived by them from that occupation; or (*b*) have been insured persons for a period of five years or upwards; and the persons possessing such qualifications who become or continue to be insured persons are in this Act referred to as voluntary contributors: Provided always that no person whose total income from all sources exceeds one hundred and sixty pounds a year shall be entitled to be a voluntary contributor unless he has been insured under this Part of this Act for a period of five years or upwards.

(4) Except as herein-after provided, nothing in this section shall require or authorise a person of the age of sixty-five or upwards not previously insured under this Part of this Act to become so insured.

2. – (1) Where any person employed within the meaning of this Part of this Act proves that he is either –

(*a*) in receipt of any pension or income of the annual value of twenty-six pounds or upwards not dependent upon his personal exertions; or

(*b*) ordinarily and mainly dependent for his livelihood upon some other person;

he shall be entitled to a certificate exempting him from the liability to become or to continue to be insured under this Part of this Act.

(2) All claims for exemption shall be made to, and certificates of exemption granted by, the Insurance Commissioners in the prescribed manner and subject to the prescribed conditions, and may be so made and granted before, as well as after, the commencement of this Act: Provided that the regulations of the Insurance Commissioners may provide for claims under this section being made to and certificates granted by approved societies and Insurance Committees herein-after constituted.

Contributions

3. Except as otherwise provided by this Act, the funds for providing the benefits conferred by this Part of this Act and defraying the expenses of the administration of those benefits shall be derived as to seven-ninths (or, in the case of women, three-fourths) thereof from contributions made by or in respect of the contributors by themselves or their employers, and as to the remaining two-ninths (or, in the case of women, one quarter) thereof from moneys provided by Parliament.

4. – (1) The contributions payable in respect of employed contributors shall be at the rate specified in Part I of the Second Schedule to this Act (herein-after referred to as the employed rate), and shall comprise contributions by the contributors and contributions by their employers at the rates specified in that Part of that schedule, and shall be payable at weekly or other prescribed intervals:

Provided that, in the case of an employed contributor of the age of twenty-one or upwards whose remuneration does not include the provision of board and lodging by the employer and the rate of whose remuneration does not exceed two shillings a working day, such part of the contributions payable in respect of him as is specified in the said schedule shall be paid out of moneys provided by Parliament.

(2) The employer shall, in the first instance, pay both the contributions payable by himself (in this Act referred to as the employer's contributions), and also on behalf of the employed contributor the contributions payable by such contributor, and shall be entitled to recover from the contributor, by deduction from his wages or otherwise the amount of the contributions so paid by him on behalf of the contributor, in accordance with the rules set out in the Third Schedule to this Act.

(3) Contributions in respect of employed contributors shall cease to be payable on their attaining the age of seventy.

(4) The employer of a person who though employed within the meaning of this Part of this Act is not insured under this Part of this Act by reason either –

(a) that, not having previously been an insured person, he has become employed within the meaning of this part of this Act after attaining the age of sixty-five; or

(b) that he has obtained and still holds a certificate of exemption under this Part of this Act;

shall be liable to pay the like contributions as would have been payable as employer's contributions if such person had been an employed contributor, and such contributions shall be carried to such account and dealt with in such manner as may be prescribed by regulations made by the Insurance Commissioners, and those regulations may provide for applying the sums standing to the credit of the account, or any part thereof, for the benefit of any persons in respect of whom contributions have been so paid, in the event of such persons subsequently becoming employed contributors. . . .

PART II. UNEMPLOYMENT INSURANCE

84. Every workman who, having been employed in a trade mentioned in the Sixth Schedule to this Act (in this Act referred to as 'an insured trade') is unemployed, and in whose case the conditions laid down by this Part of this Act (in this Act referred to as 'statutory conditions') are fulfilled, shall be entitled, subject to the provisions of this Part of this Act, to receive payments (in this Act referred to as 'unemployment benefit') at weekly or other prescribed intervals at such rates and for such periods as are authorised by or under the Seventh Schedule to this Act. . . .

85. – (1) The sums required for the payment of unemployment benefit under this Act shall be derived partly from contributions by workmen in the insured trades and partly from contributions by employers of such workmen and partly from moneys provided by Parliament.

(2) Subject to the provisions of this Part of this Act, every workman employed within the United Kingdom in an insured trade, and every employer of any such workman, shall be liable to pay contributions at the rates specified in the Eighth Schedule to this Act.

(3) Except where the regulations under this Part of this Act otherwise

prescribe, the employer shall, in the first instance, be liable to pay both the contribution payable by himself, and also on behalf of and to the exclusion of the workman, the contribution payable by such workman, and subject to such regulations, shall be entitled, notwithstanding the provisions of any Act or any contract to the contrary, to recover from the workman by deductions from the workman's wages or from any other payment due from him to the workman the amount of the contributions so paid by him on behalf of the workman.

(4) Notwithstanding any contract to the contrary, the employer shall not be entitled to deduct from the wages of or other payment due to the workman, or otherwise recover from the workman by any legal process the contributions payable by the employer himself. . . .

(6) A contribution shall be made in each year out of moneys provided by Parliament equal to one-third of the total contributions received from employers and workmen during that year, and the sums to be contributed in any year shall be paid in such manner and at such times as the Treasury may determine.

86. The statutory conditions for the receipt of unemployment benefit by any workman are –

(1) that he proves that he has been employed as a workman in an insured trade in each of not less than twenty-six separate calendar weeks in the preceding five years;

(2) That he has made application for unemployment benefit in the prescribed manner, and proves that since the date of the application he has been continuously unemployed;

(3) that he is capable of work but unable to obtain suitable employment;

(4) that he has not exhausted his right to unemployment benefit under this Part of this Act:

Provided that a workman shall not be deemed to have failed to fulfil the statutory conditions by reason only that he has declined –

(*a*) an offer of employment in a situation vacant in consequence of a stoppage of work due to a trade dispute; or

(*b*) an offer of employment in the district where he was last ordinarily employed at a rate of wage lower, or on conditions less favourable, than those which he habitually obtained in his usual employment in that district, or would have obtained had he continued to be so employed; or

(*c*) an offer of employment in any other district at a rate of wage lower or on conditions less favourable than those generally observed in such district by agreement between associations of employers and of workmen, or, failing any such agreement, than those generally recognised in such district by good employers.

87. – (1) A workman who has lost employment by reason of a stoppage of work which was due to a trade dispute at the factory, workshop, or other premises at which he was employed, shall be disqualified for receiving unemployment benefit so long as the stoppage of work continues, except in a case where he has, during the stoppage of work, become bona fide employed elsewhere in an insured trade.

Where separate branches of work which are commonly carried on as separate businesses in separate premises are in any case carried on in separate departments on the same premises, each of those departments shall, for the purposes of this provision, be deemed to be a separate factory or workshop or separate premises, as the case may be.

(2) A workman who loses employment through misconduct or who voluntarily leaves his employment without just cause shall be disqualified for receiving unemployment benefit for a period of six weeks from the date when he so lost employment.

(3) A workman shall be disqualified for receiving unemployment benefit whilst he is an inmate of any prison or any workhouse or other institution supported wholly or partly out of public funds, and whilst he is resident temporarily or permanently outside the United Kingdom.

(4) A workman shall be disqualified for receiving unemployment benefit while he is in receipt of any sickness or disablement benefit or disablement allowance under Part I, of this Act. . . .

SIXTH SCHEDULE

List of insured trades for the purposes of Part II of this Act relating to unemployment insurance

(1) Building; that is to say, the construction, alteration, repair, decoration, or demolition of buildings, including the manufacture of any fittings or wood of a kind commonly made in builders' workshops or yards.

(2) Construction of works; that is to say, the construction, reconstruction, or alteration of railroads, docks, harbours, canals, embankments, bridges, piers or other works of construction.

(3) Shipbuilding; that is to say, the construction, alteration, repair or decoration of ships, boats or other craft by persons not being usually members of a ship's crew, including the manufacture of any fittings of wood of a kind commonly made in a shipbuilding yard.

(4) Mechanical engineering, including the manufacture of ordnance and firearms.

(5) Ironfounding, whether included under the foregoing headings or not.

(6) Construction of vehicles; that is to say, the construction, repair, or decoration of vehicles.

(7) Sawmilling (including machine woodwork) carried on in connection with any other insured trade or of a kind commonly so carried on.

SEVENTH SCHEDULE

Rates and periods of unemployment benefit

In respect of each week following the first week of any period of unemployment, seven shillings, or such other rates as may be prescribed either generally or for any particular trade or any branch thereof:

Provided that, in the case of a workman under the age of eighteen, no unemployment benefit shall be paid while the workman is below the age of seventeen, and while the workman is of the age of seventeen or upwards but below the age of eighteen, unemployment benefit shall only be paid at half the rate at which it would be payable if the workman was above the age of eighteen.

No workman shall receive unemployment benefit for more than fifteen or such other number of weeks as may be prescribed either generally or for any particular trade or branch thereof within any period of twelve months, or in respect of any period less than one day.

No workman shall receive more unemployment benefit than in the proportion of one week's benefit for every five contributions paid by him under this Act:

Provided that for the purpose of the foregoing paragraph –

(*a*) in the case of a workman who satisfies the Board of Trade that he is over the age of twenty-one and has habitually worked at an insured trade before the commencement of this Act, there shall be deemed to be added to the number of contributions which he has actually paid five contributions for each period of three months or part of such period during which he has so worked before the commencement of this Act, up to a maximum of twenty-five contributions; and

(*b*) where, owing to the fact that the wages or other remuneration of a workman are paid at intervals greater than a week, or for any other like reason contributions are paid under Part II of this Act in respect of any workman at intervals greater than a week, that workman shall be entitled to treat each of such contributions as so many contributions as there are weeks in the period for which the contribution has been paid. Any time during which a workman is, under Part II of this Act, disqualified for receiving unemployment benefit shall be excluded in the computation of periods of unemployment under this schedule.

A period of unemployment shall not be deemed to commence till the workman has made application for unemployment benefit in such manner as may be prescribed.

The power conferred by this schedule on the Board of Trade to prescribe rates and periods of unemployment benefit shall not be exercised so as to increase the rate of benefit above eight shillings per week or reduce it below six shillings per week, or to increase the period of unemployment benefit above fifteen weeks, or to alter the proportion which the period of benefit bears to the number of contributions paid, except by rules confirmed by an order made in accordance with the provisions of this Act relating to special orders.

EIGHTH SCHEDULE

Contributions for the purposes of Part II of this Act relating to unemployment insurance

Rates of contribution from workmen and employers.

From every workman employed in an insured trade for every week he is so employed .... 2½d.

From every employer by whom one or more workmen are employed in an insured trade, in respect of each workman, for every week he is so employed .... 2½d.

Provided that, in the case of a workman below the age of eighteen, 1d. shall be substituted for 2½d. as the contribution from the workman and from the employer, but, for the purpose of reckoning the number of contributions in respect of such a workman except as regards the payment of unemployment benefit before he reaches the age of eighteen, the 1d. shall be treated as two-fifths of a contribution.

Every such period of employment of less than a week shall, for the purposes of this schedule, be treated as if it were employment for a whole week, except that, where the period of employment is two days or less, the contributions both of the employer and of the workman shall be reduced to one penny if the period does not exceed one day and to twopence if it exceeds one day; and, in such case, in reckoning the number of contributions under Part II of this Act and the schedules therein referred to, contributions at such reduced rates shall be treated as two-fifths of a contribution as the case may require.

(National Insurance Act, 1911)

I.24 'Socialists united, Paris' (1905)

The delegates of the French organizations – the Revolutionary Socialist Workers' Party, the Socialist Party of France, the French Socialist Party, the Independent Federations, etc. – declare that the action of the United Socialist Party must be based on the principles which have been established by the international congresses, especially the most recent ones at Paris in 1900 and at Amsterdam in 1904.

They state that the divergences of views and different interpretations of tactics, which have so far been able to appear, are due above all to circumstances peculiar to France and to the absence of a general organization.

They affirm their common desire to found a party of the class war which, even while it takes advantage for the workers of minor conflicts among the rich, or is by chance able to concert its action with that of a political party for the defence of the rights or interests of the proletariat, remains always a party of fundamental and unyielding opposition to the whole of the bourgeois class and to the State which is its instrument.

Consequently, the delegates declare that their oganizations are ready to collaborate forthwith in this work of unifying the socialist forces on the following bases:

1. The Socialist Party is a class party whose aim is to socialize the means of production and distribution, that is to transform capitalist society into a collectivist or communist society, and to adopt as its means the economic or political organization of the proletariat. By its purpose, its ideal, by the means it adopts, the Socialist Party, while pursuing the achievement of the immediate reforms claimed by the working class, is not a party of reform but a party of class war and revolution.

2. Those whom it returns to Parliament form a single group as compared with all the bourgeois political sects. The Socialist group in Parliament must refuse the Government all the resources which ensure the power of the bourgeoisie and its domination, must refuse, therefore, military credits, credits for colonial conquests, secret funds and the whole of the budget.

Even in exceptional circumstances, those returned cannot commit the Party without its consent.

In Parliament the Socialist group must dedicate itself to the defence and the extension of the political liberties and rights of the workers, to the pursuit and realization of reforms such as will improve the conditions of life and advance the struggle of the working class.

Deputies, like all other selected members, must hold themselves at the disposition of the Party, to serve its action in the country, its general propaganda for organizing the proletariat, and the final ends of socialism. . . .

[Articles 3 to 7 assert the authority of the Party over all its elected representatives and over the Party press, exacting from deputies a portion of their parliamentary salaries and obedience to a *mandat impératif* – i.e., to prior instructions given to deputies by the Party organization. The statement also proposes a Congress of Unity to be held as soon as possible.]

(Policy statement of the new united French Socialist Party, Section Française de l'Internationale Ouvrière; quoted in D. Thomson, *France: Empire and Republic, 1850–1940*, Macmillan, 1968, pp. 283–4)

I.25 The Charter of Amiens (1906)

The Confederal Congress of Amiens confirms Article 2 of the Constitution of the *Confédération Générale du Travail*: 'The CGT unites, independently of all schools of politics, all workers conscious of the need to strive for abolition of employers and wage earners.'

The Congress holds that this declaration is a recognition of the class war which, in economic life, rallies workers in revolt against all the forms of exploitation and oppression, material as well as moral, practised by the capitalist class against the working class.

The Congress adds to this affirmation of general principle the following specific points:

In the process of making its everyday demands syndicalism seeks to co-ordinate the efforts of the workers, to better their conditions through achieving such immediate improvements as shorter working hours, wage increases, etc.

But this activity is only one side of the work of syndicalism. It is preparing that complete emancipation, which can be accomplished only when the capitalist is expropriated; it commends the general strike as a means of action, and it believes that the *syndicat*, which is now the nucleus of resistance, will in future become the nucleus for production and distribution, the foundation of social reorganization.

The Congress declares that this double task of everyday life and of the future is the outcome of the conditions of wage earners which is burdensome to all workers and makes it the duty of the wage-earning class, whatever their political or philosophical inclinations, to belong to that essential group, the *syndicat*.

Accordingly, so far as individuals are concerned, the Congress declares that all members have complete freedom to take part outside the corporate group in any form of struggle which their political or philosophical beliefs may require, and it confines itself to asking them, in return, not to introduce into the *syndicat* opinions which they profess outside.

So far as organizations are concerned, the Congress decides that, for syndicalism to attain maximum effectiveness, economic action should be exercised directly against the employer class, and the Confederal Organizations must not, as syndicalist groups, pay heed to the parties and sects which, outside and by their side, are completely free to pursue their aims of social transformation.

(Charter adopted at Amiens conference of the Confédération Générale du Travail, 1906; quoted in D. Thomson, *France: Empire and Republic 1850–1940*, Macmillan, 1968, pp. 171–2)

I.26 'Appeal to the soldiers of all the belligerent countries' (1917)

Brothers, soldiers!

We are all worn out by this frightful war, which has cost millions of lives, crippled millions of people and caused untold misery, ruin, and starvation.

And more and more people are beginning to ask themselves: What started this war, what is it being waged for?

Every day it is becoming clearer to us, the workers and peasants, who bear the brunt of the war, that it was started and is being waged by the capitalists of all countries for the sake of the capitalists' interests, for the sake of world supremacy, for the sake of markets for the manufacturers, factory owners and bankers, for the sake of plundering the weak nationalities. They are carving up colonies and seizing territories in the Balkans and in Turkey – and for this the European peoples must be ruined, for this, we must die, for this we must witness the ruin, starvation and death of our families.

The capitalist class in all countries is deriving colossal, staggering, scandalously high profits from contracts and war supplies, from concessions in annexed countries, and from the rising price of goods. The capitalist class has imposed contribution on all the nations for decades ahead in the shape of high interest on the billions lent in war loans. And we, the workers and peasants, must die, suffer ruin, and starve, must patiently bear all this and strengthen our oppressors, the capitalists, by having the workers of the different countries exterminate each other and feel hatred for each other.

Are we going to continue submissively to bear our yoke, to put up with the war between the capitalist classes? Are we going to let this war drag on by taking the side of our own national governments, our own national bourgeoisies, our own national capitalists, and thereby destroying the international unity of the workers of all countries, of the whole world?

No, brother soldiers, it is time we opened our eyes, it is time we took our fate into our own hands. In all countries popular wrath against the capitalist class, which has drawn the people into the war, is growing, spreading, and gaining strength. Not only in Germany, but even in Britain, which before the war had the reputation of being one of the freest countries, hundreds and hundreds of true friends and representatives of the working class are languishing in prison for having spoken the honest truth against the war and against the capitalists. The revolution in Russia is only the first step of the first revolution; it should be followed and will be followed by others.

The new government in Russia – which has overthrown Nicholas II, who was as bad a crowned brigand as Wilhelm II – is a government of the capitalists. It is waging just as predatory and imperialist a war as the capitalists of Germany, Britain, and other countries. It has endorsed the predatory secret treaties concluded by Nicholas II with the capitalists of Britain, France, and other countries; it is not publishing these treaties for the world to know, just as the German Government is not publishing its secret and equally predatory treaties with Austria, Bulgaria, and so on. . . .

Peace to the hovels, war on the palaces! Peace to the workers of all countries! Long live the fraternal unity of the revolutionary workers of all countries! Long live socialism!

Central Committee of the RSDLP
Petrograd Committee of the RSDLP
Editorial Board of Pravda

(*Pravda*, No. 37, 4 May [21 April] 1917)

I.27 Memorandum by Prince Karl Max Lichnowsky, from J. Röhl, *1914: Delusion or Design?* (Jan. 1915)

When I arrived in London in November 1912 the First Balkan War had really already ended with the Allies' victory over Turkey, and the disposal of the Turkish heritage raised the spectre of a European war.

A few days after my arrival, Lord Haldane, a close friend of Sir E. Grey's, visited me to tell me roughly the following: England desired peace and friendship with us, and hoped with my help to strengthen our relations and to remove all misunderstandings. But he drew my attention to one important point from the first: *England could never permit the destruction or weakening of France.* This was a vital question for Great Britain. She had to support France, as we had to support Austria. The basis of any understanding with us must therefore be *an unquestionable policy of peace*, since England would be drawn through France into a European war. But England no more wished to attack us than to foster the French idea of revanche. . . .

On our side *nothing*, absolutely *nothing*, was done to preserve peace, and when we *at last* decided to do what I had advocated from the first, it was too late. By then Russia, as a result of our harsh attitude and that of Count Berchtold, had lost all confidence and mobilised. The war party gained the upper hand. . . .

Such a policy is comprehensible only if war was our aim, not otherwise.

The influential people at the [Foreign] Office repeatedly told me that Russia would be 'ready' in 1916, and that we should not wait for that. Our relations with Russia had visibly deteriorated, so much is true. But instead of trying to improve them by replacing personnel and by showing greater discretion in supporting Austrian wishes, as well as consideration for Russian sensibilities in other matters, we took up arms. Who can prove that we would really have had to fight in 1916? To what end would Russia have attacked us? *England and France were absolutely peaceable and would have remained so*; they would never have supported a Russian attack.

But the crucial questions are not: Did Grey want war? Why did he not prevent it? What did he do or not do to prevent it? – but rather: Did we want war? Why did *we* not prevent it? What did *we* do or not do to prevent it?

(J. Röhl, *1914: Delusion or Design? The Testimony of Two German Diplomats*, St. Albans, Elek, 1973)

I.28   P. N. Durnovo, memorandum to the Tsar (Feb. 1914)

[Durnovo, member of the Russian State Council and formerly head of the Police Department of the Ministry of the Interior and then Deputy Minister of the Interior, was well-known as an upholder of the status quo and opponent of both liberals and revolutionaries.]

A FUTURE ANGLO-GERMAN WAR WILL BECOME AN ARMED CONFLICT BETWEEN TWO GROUPS OF POWERS

The central factor of the period of world history through which we are now passing is the rivalry between England and Germany. This rivalry must inevitably lead to an armed struggle between them, the issue of which will, in all probability, prove fatal to the vanquished side. The interests of these two powers are far too incompatible, and their simultaneous existence as world powers will sooner or later prove impossible. On the one hand, there is an insular state, whose world importance rests upon its domination of the sea, its world trade, and its innumerable colonies. On the other, there is a powerful continental empire, whose limited territory is insufficient for an increased population. It has therefore openly and candidly declared that its future is on the seas. It has, with fabulous speed, developed an enormous world commerce, built for its protection a formidable navy, and, with its famous trademark, 'Made in Germany', created a mortal danger to the industrial and economic prosperity of its rival. Naturally, England cannot yield without a fight, and between her and Germany a struggle for life or death is inevitable.

The armed conflict impending as a result of this rivalry cannot be confined to a duel between England and Germany alone. Their resources are far too unequal, and, at the same time, they are not sufficiently vulnerable to each other. Germany could provoke rebellion in India, in South Africa, and, especially, a dangerous rebellion in Ireland, and paralyse English sea trade by means of privateering and, perhaps, submarine warfare, thereby creating for Great Britain difficulties in her food supply; but, in spite of all the daring of the German military leaders, they would scarcely risk landing in England, unless a fortunate accident helped them to destroy or appreciably to weaken the English navy. As for England, she will find Germany absolutely invulnerable. All that she may achieve is to seize the German colonies, stop German sea trade, and, in the most favourable event, annihilate the German navy, but nothing more. This, however, would not force the enemy to sue for peace. There is no doubt, therefore, that England will attempt the means she has more than once used with success, and will risk armed action only after securing participation in the war, on her own side, of powers stronger in a strategical sense. But since Germany, for her own part, will not be found isolated, the future Anglo-German war will undoubtedly be transformed into an armed conflict between two groups of powers, one with a German, the other with an English orientation. . . .

EVEN A VICTORY OVER GERMANY PROMISES RUSSIA AN EXCEEDINGLY UNFAVOURABLE PROSPECT

In any case, even if we were to admit the necessity for eradicating German domination in the field of our economic life, even at the price of a total banishment of German capital from Russian industry, appropriate measures could be taken, it would seem, without war against Germany. Such a war will demand such enormous expenditures that they will many times exceed the more than doubtful advantages to us in the abolition of the German [economic] domination. More than that, the result of such a war will be an economic situation compared with which the yoke of German capital will seem easy.

For there can be no doubt that the war will necessitate expenditures which are beyond Russia's limited financial means. We shall have to obtain credit from allied and neutral countries, but this will not be granted gratuitously. As to what will happen if the war should end disastrously for us, I do not wish to discuss now. The financial and economic consequences of defeat can be neither calculated nor foreseen, and will undoubtedly spell the total ruin of our entire national economy.

But even victory promises us extremely unfavourable financial prospects; a totally ruined Germany will not be in a position to compensate us for the cost involved. Dictated in the interest of England, the peace treaty will not afford Germany opportunity for sufficient economic recuperation to cover our war expenditures, even at a distant time. The little which we may perhaps succeed in extorting from her will have to be shared with our allies, and to our share there will fall but negligible crumbs, compared with the war cost. Meantime, we shall have to pay our war loans, not without pressure by the allies. For, after the destruction of German power, we shall no longer be necessary to them. Nay, more, our political might, enhanced by our victory, will induce them to weaken us, at least economically. And so it is inevitable that, even after a victorious conclusion of the war, we shall fall into the same sort of financial and economic dependence upon our creditors, compared with which our present dependence upon German capital will seem ideal.

However, no matter how sad may be the economic prospects which face us as a result of union with England, and, by that token, of war with Germany, they are still of secondary importance when we think of the political consequences of this fundamentally unnatural alliance.

A STRUGGLE BETWEEN RUSSIA AND GERMANY IS
PROFOUNDLY UNDESIRABLE TO BOTH SIDES, AS IT AMOUNTS
TO A WEAKENING OF THE MONARCHIST PRINCIPLE

It should not be forgotten that Russia and Germany are the representatives of the conservative principle in the civilized world, as opposed to the
democratic principle, incarnated in England and, to an infinitively lesser
degree, in France. Strange as it may seem, England, monarchistic and
conservative to the marrow at home, has in her foreign relations always
acted as the protector of the most demagogical tendencies, invariably
encouraging all popular movements aiming at the weakening of the
monarchical principle.

From this point of view, a struggle between Germany and Russia,
regardless of its issue, is profoundly undesirable to both sides, as undoubtedly involving the weakening of the conservative principle in the
world of which the above-named two great powers are the only reliable
bulwarks. More than that, one must realize that under the exceptional
conditions which exist, a general European war is mortally dangerous
both for Russia and Germany, no matter who wins. It is our firm
conviction, based upon a long and careful study of all contemporary
subversive tendencies, that there must inevitably break out in the defeated country a social revolution which, by the very nature of things, will
spread to the country of the victor.

During the many years of peaceable neighbourly existence, the two
countries have become united by many ties, and a social upheaval in one
is bound to affect the other. That these troubles will be of a social, and not
a political, nature cannot be doubted, and this will hold true, not only as
regards Russia, but for Germany as well. An especially favourable soil for
social upheavals is found in Russia, where the masses undoubtedly
profess, unconsciously, the principles of Socialism. In spite of the spirit of
antagonism to the Government in Russian society, as unconscious as the
Socialism of the broad masses of the people, a political revolution is not
possible in Russia, and any revolutionary movement inevitably must
degenerate into a Socialist movement. The opponents of the government
have no popular support. The people see no difference between a
government official and an intellectual. The Russian masses, whether
workmen or peasants, are not looking for political rights, which they
neither want nor comprehend.

The peasant dreams of obtaining a gratuitous share of somebody else's
land; the workman, of getting hold of the entire capital and profits of the
manufacturer. Beyond this, they have no aspirations. If these slogans are
scattered far and wide among the populace, and the Government permits
agitation along these lines, Russia will be flung into anarchy, such as she
suffered in the ever-memorable period of troubles in 1905–1906. War with
Germany would create exceptionally favourable conditions for such
agitation. As already stated, this war is pregnant with enormous diffi-

culties for us, and cannot turn out to be a mere triumphal march to Berlin. Both military disasters – partial ones, let us hope – and all kinds of shortcomings in our supply are inevitable. In the excessive nervousness and spirit of opposition of our society, these events will be given an exaggerated importance, and all the blame will be laid on the Government.

It will be well if the Government does not yield, but declares directly that in time of war no criticism of the governmental authority is to be tolerated, and resolutely suppresses all opposition.

(Frank Golder (ed.) *Documents of Russian History, 1914–1917*, trans. Emanuel Aronsberg, New York, Century, 1927)

II
WORLD WAR I AND ITS
CONSEQUENCES

II.1 Extracts from New York *Tribune* (25/26, 27 April 1915)

North of France, April 24. – There is no doubt that the action which has been proceeding about Ypres for a week, and which will probably be known in history as the second battle of Ypres, is the hardest and hottest which has yet developed on the extreme Western front. Indeed, no battle of the war has developed so much action on so concentrated a front. It is the third desperate attempt of the Germans since this war began to break through the combined British and Belgian lines and take the all-important City of Calais.

This series of attacks and counterattacks running along the whole line, developed into that general attack on the British lines with Calais for objective which the Germans probably had been planning ever since matters began to come to a deadlock in the Carpathians. The Germans, making full use of their artillery, launched infantry attacks in their old manner – close-locked. As formerly, the British and French slaughtered them heavily with machine-gun and rifle fire. Then on Thursday the Germans suddenly threw in that attack its asphyxiating bombs, which will doubtless become famous in this war. It succeeded in breaking the line of French near Bixschoote, although not to such an extent as the Germans claim in today's communiqué.

The nearest British support was a part of the Canadian contingent. Fighting with desperate bravery, the Canadians succeeded in recovering part of the lost ground.

◆　◆　◆

They are still at it today. On a favourable wind the sound of cannonading can be heard as far away as the coast towns.

The nature of the gases carried by the German asphyxiating shells remain a mystery. Whatever gas it is, it spreads rapidly and remains close to the ground. It is believed not to be specially deadly – one that rather overpowers its victims and puts them *hors de combat* without killing many. Its effect at Bixschoote may have been due to panic caused by the novelty of the device. Its composition and manner of discharge are probably no mystery to the scientific artillerymen of the Allies. That such devices might be used in war has been known for a long time, but the positive prohibitions of The Hague Conference have prevented the more civilized nations of Europe from going far with experiments in this line.

Boulogne, April 25. – The gaseous vapor which the Germans used against the French divisions near Ypres last Thursday, contrary to the rules of The Hague Convention, introduces a new element into warfare. The attack of last Thursday evening was preceded by the rising of a cloud of vapor, greenish grey and iridescent. That vapor settled to the ground like a swamp mist and drifted toward the French trenches on a brisk wind. Its effect on the French was a violent nausea and faintness, followed by an utter collapse. It is believed that the Germans, who charged in behind the vapor, met no resistance at all, the French at their front being virtually paralyzed.

Everything indicates long and thorough preparation for this attack. The work of sending out the vapor was done from the advanced German trenches. Men garbed in a dress resembling the harness of a diver and armed with retorts or generators about three feet high and connected with ordinary hose pipe turned the vapor loose towards the French lines. Some witnesses maintain that the Germans sprayed the earth before the trenches with a fluid which, being ignited, sent up the fumes. The German troops, who followed up this advantage with a direct attack, held inspirators in their mouths, thus preventing them from being overcome by the fumes.

In addition to this, the Germans appear to have fired ordinary explosive shells loaded with some chemical which had a paralyzing effect on all the men in the region of the explosion. Some chemical in the composition of those shells produced violent watering of the eyes, so that the men overcome by them were practically blinded for some hours.

The effect of the noxious trench gas seems to be slow in wearing away. The men come out of their nausea in a state of utter collapse. Some of the rescued have already died from the after-effects. How many of the men left unconscious in the trenches when the French broke died from the fumes it is impossible to say, since those trenches were at once occupied by the Germans.

This new form of attack needs for success a favourable wind. Twice in the day that followed the Germans tried trench vapor on the Canadians, who made on the right of the French position a stand which will probably be remembered as one of the heroic episodes of this war. In both cases the wind was not favourable, and the Canadians managed to stick through it. The noxious, explosive bombs were, however, used continually against the Canadian forces and caused some losses.

(Louis L. Snyder (ed.) *Historic Documents of World War I*, Princeton, New Jersey, Van Nostrand Reinhold Co., 1958)

II.2 'Programme of the Union of Economic Interests [an employers' organization]' (7 April 1919)

1. Defence of property and of private enterprise. Freedom of agriculture, commerce, industry and labour. Protection of commercial property.

2. Formal opposition to any creation of new monopolies, to any experiments in collectivist socialization, to all control by the State over any services of a commercial or industrial character, to the exploitation by the State of services presently in its hands, and in general to all interference by the State in the running of private undertakings.

The end of State consortiums.

More efficient organization of existing monopolies, the present management of which conflicts with the interests of the public and of the Treasury.

3. The obligation of the State to observe the contracts it has signed. An embargo on the introduction of new charges without the consent of those holding contracts and without prior agreement as to compensation.

Reassertion of the principle forbidding retrospective legislation. . . .

6. . . . Compulsory and enforceable consultation of mandated representatives from the legally constituted Chambers of Commerce, Professional Bodies, and Groups of Economic Interests in all projects and legislative proposals relating to the economic life of the country.

7. The union of Capital and Labour. Co-operation among employers and industrial and white-collar workers. Resolution of matters of concern in a spirit of unity, liberty and peace.

8. Co-ordination of social welfare legislation taking account of the economic needs of different regions and employers.

Effective application of the weekly day of rest.

9. Administrative reorganization and decentralization in face of the advance of national and regional initiatives.

10. Organization of technical education and apprenticeship in collaboration with interested professional organizations.

11. Assistance to large families.

Action against depopulation and all of its causes: tuberculosis, slum housing, alcohol abuse, etc. Proper enforcement of all existing legislation aimed at the suppression of public drunkenness.

12. Adoption of a legislative decree forbidding withdrawal of labour in any public service, whether run by the State or by a private concession.

(Georges Lefranc, *Les organisations patronales en France*, Paris, Payot, 1976, pp. 328–9; trans. A. Marwick)

II.3   From the Treaty of Versailles (1919)

ARTICLE 88

Annex

1.

Within fifteen days from the coming into force of the present Treaty the German troops and such officials as may be designated by the Commission set up under the provisions of paragraph 2 shall evacuate the plebiscite area. Up to the moment of the completion of the evacuation they shall refrain from any form of requisitioning in money or in kind and from all acts likely to prejudice the material interests of the country.

Within the same period the Workmens' and Soldiers' Councils which have been constituted in this area shall be dissolved. Members of such Councils who are natives of another region and are exercising their functions at the date of the coming into force of the present Treaty, or who have gone out of office since March 1, 1919, shall be evacuated.

All military and semi-military unions formed in the said area by inhabitants of the district shall be immediately disbanded. All members of such military organizations who are not domiciled in the said area shall be required to leave it.

2.

The plebiscite area shall be immediately placed under the authority of an International Commission of four members to be designated by the following Powers; the United States of America, France, the British Empire and Italy. It shall be occupied by troops belonging to the Allied and Associated Powers, and the German Government undertakes to give facilities for the transference of these troops to Upper Silesia.

3.

The Commission shall enjoy all the powers exercised by the German or the Prussian Government, except those of legislation or taxation. It shall also be substituted for the government of the province and the *Regierungsbezirk*.

It shall be within the competence of the Commission to interpret the powers hereby conferred upon it and to determine to what extent it shall exercise them, and to what extent they shall be left in the hands of the existing authorities.

Changes in the existing laws and the existing taxation shall only be brought into force with the consent of the Commission.

The Commission will maintain order with the help of the troops which will be at its disposal, and, to the extent which it may deem necessary, by means of gendarmerie recruited among the inhabitants of the country.

The Commission shall provide immediately for the replacement of the evacuated German officials and, if occasion arises, shall itself order the evacuation of such authorities and proceed to the replacement of such local authorities as may be required.

It shall take all steps which it thinks proper to ensure the freedom, fairness and secrecy of the vote. In particular, it shall have the right to order the expulsion of any person who may in any way have attempted to distort the result of the plebiscite by methods of corruption or intimidation.

The Commission shall have full power to settle all questions arising from the execution of the present clauses. It shall be assisted by technical advisers chosen by it from among the local population.

The decisions of the Commission shall be taken by a majority vote.

4.

The vote shall take place at such date as may be determined by the Principal Allied and Associated Powers, but not sooner than six months or later than eighteen months after the establishment of the Commission in the area.

The right to vote shall be given to all persons without distinction of sex who:

(*a*) Have completed their twentieth year on the 1st January of the year in which the plebiscite takes place;

(*b*) Were born in the plebiscite area or have been domiciled there since a date to be determined by the Commission, which shall not be subsequent to the 1st January, 1919, or who have been expelled by the German authorities and have not retained their domicile there.

Persons convicted of political offences shall be enabled to exercise their right of voting.

Every person will vote in the commune where he is domiciled or in which he was born, if he has not retained his domicile in the area.

The result of the vote will be determined by communes according to the majority of votes in each commune.

5.

On the conclusion of the voting, the number of votes cast in each commune will be communicated by the Commission to the Principal Allied and Associated Powers, with a full report as to the taking of the vote and a recommendation as to the line which ought to be adopted as the frontier of Germany in Upper Silesia. In this recommendation regard will be paid to the wishes of the inhabitants as shown by the vote, and to the geographical and economic conditions of the locality.

6.

As soon as the frontier has been fixed by the Principal Allied and Associated Powers, the German authorities will be notified by the International Commission that they are free to take over the administration of the territory which it is recognised should be German; the said authorities must proceed to do so within one month of such notification and in the manner prescribed by the Commission.

Within the same period and in the manner prescribed by the Commission, the Polish Government must proceed to take over the administration of the territory which it is recognised should be Polish.

When the administration of the territory has been provided for by the German and Polish authorities respectively, the powers of the Commission will terminate.

The cost of the army of occupation, and expenditure by the Commission, whether in discharge of its own functions or in the administration of the territory, will be a charge on the area. . . .

ARTICLE 91

German nationals habitually resident in territories recognized as forming part of Poland will acquire Polish nationality *ipso facto* and will lose their German nationality.

German nationals, however, or their descendants who became resident in these territories after January 1, 1908, will not acquire Polish nationality without a special authorization from the Polish State.

Within a period of two years after the coming into force of the present Treaty, German nationals over 18 years of age habitually resident in any of the territories recognized as forming part of Poland will be entitled to opt for German nationality.

Poles who are German nationals over 18 years of age and habitually resident in Germany will have a similar right to opt for Polish nationality.

Option by a husband will cover his wife and option by parents will cover their children under 18 years of age.

Persons who have exercised the above right to opt may within the succeeding twelve months transfer their place of residence to the State for which they have opted.

They will be entitled to retain their immovable property in the territory of the other State where they had their place of residence before exercising the right to opt.

They may carry with them their movable property of every description. No export or import duties or charges may be imposed upon them in connection with the removal of such property.

Within the same period Poles who are German nationals and are in a foreign country will be entitled, in the absence of any provisions to the contrary in the foreign law, and if they have not acquired the foreign nationality, to obtain Polish nationality and to lose their German nationality by complying with the requirements laid down by the Polish State.

In the portion of Upper Silesia submitted to a plebiscite the provisions of this Article shall only come into force as from the definitive attribution of the territory.

ARTICLE 92

The proportion and the nature of the financial liabilities of Germany and Prussia which are to be borne by Poland will be determined in accordance with Article 254 of Part IX (Financial Clauses) of the present Treaty.

There shall be excluded from the share of such financial liabilities assumed by Poland that portion of the debt which, according to the finding of the Reparation Commission referred to in the above-mentioned Article, arises from measures adopted by the German and Prussian Governments with a view to German colonization in Poland.

In fixing under Article 256 of the present Treaty the value of the property and possessions belonging to the German Empire and to the German States which pass to Poland with the territory transferred above, the Reparation Commission shall exclude from the valuation buildings, forests and other State property which belonged to the former Kingdom of Poland; Poland shall acquire these properties free of all costs and charges.

In all the German territory transferred in accordance with the present Treaty and recognized as forming definitively part of Poland, the property, rights and interests of German nationals shall not be liquidated under Article 297 by the Polish Government except in accordance with the following provisions:

1. The proceeds of the liquidation shall be paid direct to the owner;

2. If on his application the Mixed Arbitral Tribunal provided for by Section VI of Part X (Economic Clauses) of the present Treaty, or an arbitrator appointed by that Tribunal, is satisfied that the conditions of the sale or measures taken by the Polish Government outside its general legislation were unfairly prejudicial to the price obtained, they shall have discretion to award to the owner equitable compensation to be paid by the Polish Government.

Further agreements will regulate all questions arising out of the cession of the above territory which are not regulated by the present Treaty.

ARTICLE 93

Poland accepts and agrees to embody in a Treaty with the Principal Allied and Associated Powers such provisions as may be deemed necessary by the said Powers to protect the interests of inhabitants of Poland who differ from the majority of the population in race, language or religion.

Poland further accepts and agrees to embody in a Treaty with the said Powers such provisions as they may deem necessary to protect freedom of transit and equitable treatment of the commerce of other nations. . . .

ARTICLE 231

The Allied and Associated Governments affirm and Germany accepts the responsibility of Germany and her allies for causing all the loss and damage to which the Allied and Associated Governments and their nationals have been subjected as a consequence of the war imposed upon them by the aggression of Germany and her allies. . . .

[The following preamble and articles 387, 388, 390 and 427 are from Part XIII of the Treaty on 'Labour'.]

Whereas the League of Nations has for its object the establishment of universal peace, and such a peace can be established only if it is based upon social justice;

And whereas conditions of labour exist involving such injustice, hardship and privation to large numbers of people as to produce unrest so great that the peace and harmony of the world are imperilled; and an improvement of those conditions is urgently required: as, for example, by the regulation of the hours of work, including the establishment of a maximum working day and week, the regulation of the labour supply, the prevention of unemployment, the provision of an adequate living wage, the protection of the worker against sickness, disease and injury arising out of his employment, the protection of children, young persons and women, provision for old age and injury, protection of the interests of workers when employed in countries other than their own, recognition of the principle of freedom of association, the organization of vocational and technical education and other measures;

Whereas also the failure of any nation to adopt humane conditions of labour is an obstacle in the way of other nations which desire to improve the conditions in their own countries;

The HIGH CONTRACTING PARTIES, moved by sentiments of justice and humanity, as well as by the desire to secure the permanent peace of the world, agree to the following. . . .

ARTICLE 387

A permanent organization is hereby established for the promotion of the objects set forth in the Preamble.

The original Members of the League of Nations shall be the original Members of this organization, and hereafter membership of the League of Nations shall carry with it membership of the said organization.

ARTICLE 388

The permanent organization shall consist of:

1. a General Conference of Representatives of the Members and,

2. an International Labour Office controlled by the Governing Body described in Article 393. . . .

ARTICLE 390

Every Delegate shall be entitled to vote individually on all matters which are taken into consideration by the Conference.

If one of the Members fails to nominate one of the non-Government Delegates whom it is entitled to nominate, the other non-Government Delegate shall be allowed to sit and speak at the Conference, but not to vote. . . .

ARTICLE 427

The High Contracting Parties, recognizing that the well-being, physical, moral and intellectual, of industrial wage-earners is of supreme international importance, have framed, in order to further this great end, the permanent machinery provided for in Section I and associated with that of the League of Nations.

They recognize that differences of climate, habits and customs, of economic opportunity and industrial tradition, make strict uniformity in the conditions of labour difficult of immediate attainment. But, holding as they do, that labour should not be regarded merely as an article of commerce they think that there are methods and principles for regulating labour conditions which all industrial communities should endeavour to apply, so far as their special circumstances will permit.

Among these methods and principles, the following seem to the High Contracting Parties to be of special and urgent importance:

First. – The guiding principle above enunciated that labour should not be regarded merely as a commodity or article of commerce.

Second. – The right of association for all lawful purposes by the employed as well as by the employers.

Third. – The payment to the employed of a wage adequate to maintain a reasonable standard of life as this is understood in their time and country.

Fourth. – The adoption of an eight hours day or a forty-eight hours week as the standard to be aimed at where it has not already been attained.

Fifth. – The adoption of a weekly rest of at least twenty-four hours, which should include Sunday wherever practicable.

Sixth. – The abolition of child labour and the imposition of such limitations on the labour of young persons as shall permit the continuation of their education and assure their proper physical development.

Seventh. – The principle that men and women should receive equal remuneration for work of equal value.

Eighth. – The standard set by law in each country with respect to the conditions of labour should have due regard to the equitable economic treatment of all workers lawfully resident therein.

Ninth. – Each State should make provision for a system of inspection in which women should take part, in order to ensure the enforcement of the laws and regulations for the protection of the employed.

Without claiming that these methods and principles are either complete or final, the High Contracting Parties are of opinion that they are well fitted to guide the policy of the League of Nations; and that, if adopted by the industrial communities who are members of the League, and safe-guarded in practice by an adequate system of such inspection, they will confer lasting benefits upon the wage-earners of the world.

(The Treaty of Versailles, 1919)

II.4 From the Care of Mothers and Young Children Act (1915)

An Act to extend the Notification of Births Act, 1907, to Areas in which it has not been adopted, and to make further provisions in connection therewith for the Care of Mothers and Young Children. [29th July 1915]

[. . .]

2. - (1) Any local authority within the meaning of the principal Act . . . may, for the purpose of the care of expectant mothers, nursing mothers, and young children, exercise any powers which a sanitary authority has in the Public Health Acts, 1875 to 1907, or the Public Health (London) Act, 1891, as the case requires.

(2) Any expenses incurred in the exercise of these powers shall be defrayed in the same manner as expenses of the local authority are defrayed in the principal Act.

Any such powers may be exercised in such manner as the authority directs by a committee or committees which shall include women and may comprise, if it is thought fit, persons who are not members of the authority. Any such committee may be empowered by the authority by which it is appointed to incur expenses up to a limit for the time being fixed by the authority, and, if so empowered, shall report any expenditure by them to the authority in such manner and at such times as the authority may direct. . . .

(Care of Mothers and Young Children Act, 1915)

II.5 'Memorandum of the Neukölln Municipal Council to the War Food Department' (3 Dec. 1917)

The increasing disquiet among our population and particularly among workmen employed in munition factories induces us to draw attention to the conditions of food supply. Remedial measures are urgently necessary, for the existing state of food distribution is according to our conviction the primary cause of the prevailing discontent.

At Neukölln about 1,300 establishments are employed on war work. Of these about 350 employ more than 50 persons each. Six of them employ more than 1,000 persons each. Following the example of great industrial concerns (such as those of Krupp, the AEG, Borsig, etc.) the larger establishments at Neukölln have employed agents to purchase foodstuffs, which they sold to their workpeople in order to supplement the official rations. Generally, these purchasing agents paid more than the official maximum prices in order to secure the commodities. In reselling foodstuffs to their workpeople some of the firms distributed them at the maximum retail prices and had, therefore, to defray the difference from their own funds. Other firms sold the goods at cost price and thereby violated the order fixing maximum prices. The result of this practice in the large munition works has been that the owners of small concerns engaged on war contracts have presented demands to the communal authorities that similar advantages in the procuring of food supplies should be secured for their employees also. These firms declare their inability to effect purchases; for, as a rule, the question of delivery by trucks is involved, and these vehicles are not so accessible to them as they are to the large firms, the latter being usually backed up by the Central Purchase Company and by government departments. The military inspecting officers support the petition of the smaller firms; and in order to obviate causes of unrest among the workpeople, the Town Council has felt compelled to purchase foodstuffs in the open market so as to place them at the disposal of these firms for distribution. In these cases, also, it has become necessary to exceed the maximum prices. The supplies obtained by the Town Council consisted, for the most part, of imported goods. To enable the Town Council to procure supplies by legal means, application was repeatedly made for import permits; but these were refused. By means of the measures adopted by the Town Council, on the recommendation of the local organizations, it was found possible to raise the workers employed at small shops to an approximate equality with those employed in the large establishments. Though the Town Council did not succeed in giving perfect satisfaction – for some inequality persists – it is able to claim at least that it has allayed the general discontent among workpeople. Until the beginning of October, therefore, conditions were fairly satisfactory. Since that time, much discontent has been manifested, because the large establishments, recognizing the increasing scarcity of food, have got hold of all the stocks within their reach. Many urban authorities have followed this example, and those communes which have striven to observe the provisions of the pertinent decrees (at least in matters of primary importance) find themselves confronted with an insoluble problem as regards their future supply of food. To this position we have been brought in consequence of the complete collapse of the economic system of the government departments. This assertion we proceed to demonstrate in regard to various foodstuffs in the paragraphs which follow:

(a) *Corn and flour supply*. The system for supplying corn or flour, it must be recognized, has been founded on a solid basis, so far as consignments to the communal unions are concerned. The only loophole in the organization is the arrangement for dealing with the seed corn of individual farms. These exceptional arrangements conduce to the result that very large quantities of grain still find their way into unregulated commerce. From aggressive merchants the council receives, in large numbers, offers of seed-corn licenses. Some of these offers are for quantities as large as 3,000 metric centners, or even more. For wheat, oats, and barley, the price asked is as much as 200 marks, the recognized trade price being only 100 marks. These offers are by no means fictitious; on the contrary, if contracts were concluded, deliveries would be well assured.

(b) *Leguminous produce*. Seed peas, beans, horse beans, and vetches are offered to the council at prices ranging between 140 and 260 marks per centner, no seed licences being annexed. As the price of 240 marks asked by one merchant seemed to the council to be too high, we declined the offer; and then another of the Greater Berlin Municipal Authorities accepted it. The quantity, in this case, was 3,100 centners, and the occasion of extortion complaints was the arrangement in regard to seed. . . .

The maximum price fixed for beet is 1.75 marks; but to this nobody pays any heed. The market price at which beet is quite openly bought and sold may be quoted. A few weeks ago this market price for beet was 3.60 marks; and subsequently it has advanced to 4.75 or even 5 marks. The maximum price of horse beans being 30 marks, the smugglers' price is 110 marks a centner. The maximum price of vetches being 28 marks, supplies are offered at 100 and 105 marks.

This panorama is on exhibition in every borough and in every industrial district, more or less prominently. Competition exists between industrial concerns and those towns in which no food is produced, and this competition is recklessly exploited by extortioners. The latter find their advantage in the fact that those with whom they do business, while conscious of the illegality of their procedure, conspire to keep silence. Hence the extortioners can always allege, without fear of contradiction, that such and such a town council has already paid so much in excess of the maximum price. Should anybody take the trouble to find out the exact truth he will get no trustworthy information. Furthermore, the representatives of communal authorities will persist in the denial of facts unless and until they can be confronted with indisputable evidence. At a meeting of the Distribution Board of Greater Berlin, held before the president in the office of the Vegetable Control Board, it was ascertained, after a long debate, that every communal authority represented at the meeting had exceeded the maximum prices in purchasing vegetables. Charlottenburg claimed commendation because in purchasing supplies from producers it had not exceeded the prices payable to wholesale dealers. Town Councils which do not commit these illegalities run the risk that their burgesses will be worse off in regard to food supplies than those of towns where the councils betake themselves to forbidden paths.

The Town Council is convinced that it has, by the foregoing statements, shown the necessity for the application of amendments to the food supply system; that in particular the system of concluding contracts with producers is entirely ineffective for insuring an equitable distribution of foodstuffs; and that smuggling can be suppressed only by subjecting all foodstuffs to official embargo, so that no foodstuffs shall be subject to a mixed system of regulated and unregulated trade. The mixed system simply prepares the way for extortion, since unrestricted dealers pounce on the foodstuffs not subject to embargo and drive prices upward, the consequence being that commodities find their way to the places where most money can be obtained.

Shortage and famine (as ancient experience proves, and as the war has demonstrated afresh) may be endured with comparative ease when brought about by sheer necessity and when the victims are convinced that their fellow-mortals are subject to the same calamity. But resentment is aroused when the facts of the case are otherwise. Hence an equitable distribution of existing foodstuffs is imperatively necessary at the present time. That this end can be attained merely by the issue of orders and the threat of penalties seems in view of actual experience to be a highly doubtful proposition, since the authorities themselves find it necessary to ignore their own orders so as to effect some improvement in the distribution of supplies – such an improvement being unattainable through legal methods. The Town Council is of opinion that an advantageous rearrangement can result only from a general seizure of all foodstuffs in the localities where they are produced. This seizure should not be executed merely by the agency of interested persons – such persons as generally compose the war companies – but by impartial vigilance committees. For this reason the Town Council brings forward the following proposals for alleviating popular discontent:

(a) Places where foodstuffs are produced, associations of dealers, the homes of producers, distribution boards, etc., should be placed under the supervision of a Vigilance Committee, consisting of six members, of whom at least four should belong to consumers' districts. So far as the delivery of field products is concerned, the consumers' representatives should consist of persons selected from the districts of the organizations requiring commodities. For all matters concerning industrial products, the consumers' representatives should be selected from the trade unions of the branch of industry concerned. The Vigilance Committee in the rural districts from which foodstuffs are obtained should act as an advisory and controlling body for the District Commissioner, while in the industrial districts it should act in a similar capacity for the head of the competent distribution board or war company. The decisions of the Vigilance Committee should be obligatory on the heads of boards controlling producers, dealers, and distributors, subject to any statutory right of objection appertaining to them. All objections to the decisions of the Vigilance Committee should be decided finally by the War Food Department.

(b) All foodstuffs should be commandeered and then transferred to demand offices for warehousing and distribution. Stocks of seeds should be safeguarded by the Vigilance Committee and distributed in accordance with the needs of cultivators.

(c) In large residential and industrial districts foodstuffs should be distributed in uniform quantities and according to a uniform system. For this purpose uniform food distribution boards should be set up for these districts, and particularly for residential and industrial districts that are closely interdependent.

The Town Council expects that in view of the present intolerable state of things – one that must inevitably precipitate a catastrophe – the War

Food Department will adopt suitable measures, at the earliest possible moment, to insure the alleviation of the causes of discontent. The urban authorities of Neukölln by unanimous resolution have declared that they regard it as a primary duty to see that a supply of food shall without fail be within the reach of their population. They have declared further that in order to insure this they are disposed to pursue the illegal methods already adopted unless the War Food Department immediately provides a remedy, and indeed even if the economic ruin of the borough should be brought about by the payment of extortionate prices which the council will not be able to transfer to the shoulders of the poorer section of the burgesses.

The council asks for an opportunity of sending a deputation consisting of six members to discuss orally the prevalent state of distress.

THE ADMINISTRATIVE BOARD
THE MUNICIPAL COUNCIL

(R. L. Lutz, *Fall of the German Empire, 1914–18*, Palo Alto, Stanford University Press, 1932, pp. 177–8, 184–6)

II.6 Report of schoolmaster from Mazerolles, Charente (1915–16)

During the first year everything went more or less well: mobilization had left us with enough men, and the harvesting and ploughing were done everywhere in time. But by the second year there were already some properties without farmers, and at the beginning of the third year, there were four abandoned properties in this commune. This is obviously disappointing, but if we recall that the younger classes, the last of the reservists, the auxiliaries declared unfit for active service, etc., had been called up by this time, so that the only hands left were old men, the situation may be said to be as good as human effort could hope to make it, the more so as agricultural machinery cannot be used in our hilly country. On those farms which have not been abandoned all the fields have been ploughed and sown: but they have not been dressed properly. The women and children have done the best they could. Those men who have not been called up never grudged their help. It is also true to say that agricultural exemptions, granted largely to the auxiliaries and as a last resort to reservists at the front, proved invaluable: soldiers on leave did the ploughing and the reaping, work impossible for women. Agricultural labourers are very scarce, and the cost of manpower reflects this fact: up to 8 and 10 francs per day for reaping. Complete hostility towards the use of German prisoners of war.

(J-J. Becker, *The Great War and the French People*, Leamington Spa, Berg, 1985, pp. 126–7)

II.7 Department of Charente: the cost of living (price changes in basic commodities, in francs) (15 Feb. 1920)

	1914	1915	1916	1917	1918	1919	1920
Bread (per ½ kg)	0.15	0.15	0.20	0.25	0.25	0.30	0.50
Meat:							
beef, veal, mutton (good cuts)	1.25	1.25	1.50	2	4	5	5
Wine (per 100 litres)	20	60	80	100	110	125	125
Sugar (per ½ kg)	0.80	0.80	0.90	0.95	1.15	1.25	1.25
Cheese (Gruyère, Roquefort) (per ½ kg)	1.50	1.50	5	6	7	7	7
Butter (per ½ kg)	1.60	1.75	—	—	—	8	8
Eggs (per dozen)	1	1.20	3	5	6	8	6
Milk (per litre)	0.10	0.10	0.15	0.30	0.40	0.60	0.75
Coffee (per ½ kg)	5	3	3.50	4	4.50	5	5
Dried beans (standard)	0.25	0.25	0.40	0.60	0.75	1.50	1.50
Split peas (per ½ kg)	0.50	—	—	—	3	3.25	3.25
Lentils (per ½ kg)	0.40	—	—	—	—	2.90	2.90
Chickens (per ½ kg)	1.25	1.50	2	3	4	4.50	4.50
Paraffin (per litre)	0.40	0.55	0.65	1	1.10	0.90	0.80
Petrol (per litre)	0.30	0.80	1	1.40	1.50	1.40	1.40
Coal (per tonne)	55	60	70	115	130	110	140
Charcoal (per 10 kg)	7	10	25	30	40	35	35
A suit	70	200	250	300	325	400	400
A pair of shoes (men's)	20	35	40	45	50	80	80
Chalk (per box)	0.75	—	—	—	1.75	2	2
Steel nibs (per box)	1.30	3	3.75	4	5.50	7	7
School books	1	1.25	1.50	1.75	2	2	2
Potatoes	0.05	0.05	0.10	0.30	0.40	0.25	0.25
An ordinary workhorse	800	—	—	—	—	3,000 to 4,000	—
A milch cow	200	—	—	—	—	1,500 to 1,800	—
A pair of working oxen	1,200	—	—	—	—	6,000 to 7,000	—
A fat pig	120	—	—	—	—	800	—
A sucking pig	30	—	—	—	—	150	—

(J-J. Becker, *The Great War and the French People*, Leamington Spa, Berg, 1985, p. 128)

II.8 'War-Industry Committees and labour participation' (1915)

(a) ORGANIZATION OF THE WAR-INDUSTRY COMMITTEES

On September 9 [1915], His Majesty confirmed the following regulations, recommended by the Council of Ministers, relating to the War-Industry Committees:

1. To help government organizations supply the army and navy with all necessary military and food supplies, there are being formed, for the duration of the war, central, regional, and local war-industry committees.

2. The war-industry committees are public organizations which have no commercial aims. Consequently economic institutions belonging to them furnish military and food supplies at cost. When placing orders with private industries and business houses, the committees, to cover general expenses, may have a rebate, the amount of which to be determined by the committees with the factories and business houses, but in no case is it to be more than one per cent of the cost of the order.

3. The composition, resources, relations [with other institutions] and activities of the Central War-Industry Committee are determined by the committee itself. The composition, resources, relations and activities of regional and local committees are determined by these committees in accordance with the general principles of organization and activities of war-industry committees, in agreement with the Central War-Industry Committee.

4. The relations between government institutions and war-industry committees in the manner of supplying the army and navy with military and food supplies is determined by mutual agreement between the committees and the military and civil authorities concerned.

5. The Central War-Industry Committee has the right to take over every kind of movable and unmovable property; to conclude contracts with private individuals, with government and public institutions; to assume all kinds of obligations; in particular, to carry out government orders for supplies and work; to organize, in agreement with the Ministries of War and Navy, methods of receiving and delivering war materials, etc.; to sue and be sued. Similar rights are enjoyed by the regional committees, organized and confirmed by the Central War-Industry Committee, as well as the local committees, organized and confirmed by the regional committees.

6. All money, property, and resources in the hands of the war-industry committees at the time of their liquidation go to the State.

(b) LABOUR PARTICIPATION IN THE WAR-INDUSTRY COMMITTEES

Petrograd. On September 10, [1915] there was the first pre-election meeting of the workmen in the factory, 'Novyi Lessner'. At the end of the day's work, the day shift packed the court of the factory and notified the management that they were to take up the question of electing delegates to the Central War-Industry Committee. The management told the men to go ahead, and they immediately elected a presiding officer.

It has been a long time since the capital witnessed such a large gathering. The night shift, instead of going to work, joined the day shift at the meeting. There were present about 4,000 workmen. After explaining the origin of the war-industry committees, the chairman proposed that the workmen should give serious thought to the idea of labour participation in the mobilization of industry, and speak out freely before the election whether it was possible or necessary to have the elections.

After this talk, and as the discussion was about to begin, something happened. The gates of the factory flew open, the mounted police rode in and told the workmen to disperse.

Those in charge of the meeting explained to the police officers that it was a legal assembly, called at the request of the Central War-Indusry Committee. The police were not satisfied. A. I. Guchkov [President of the Central War-Industry Committee], members of the *Duma*, and others were called by telephone and, finally, through their mediation, the police allowed the meeting to go on, but remained to listen.

Representatives of the two wings of the Social-Democrats [Mensheviks and Bolsheviks] and of the Narodniks [Socialist-Revolutionists] made speeches.

All agreed that the workmen should have the right to organize, that it was necessary to have unions, co-operatives, etc., to fight the high cost of living. But when it came to questions in which Marxists' and Narodniks' doctrines were involved, they disagreed. The Bolsheviks favoured taking part in the primary election but opposed participating in the final. Instead of voting at that time they proposed to proclaim their programme.* The Mensheviks took the stand that the workmen should take a broader view, make use of the elections to form factory and municipal committees, and attempt to call a labour congress, etc. The Narodniks, though not advocating any particular programme, were yet not in favour of participating beyond electing delegates.

By the time it came to the resolutions, it was already ten o'clock. The political demands were accepted, with the exception of the point relating to a responsible ministry, which the majority did not support. It was

*There were two elections. In the first one every factory having no less than five hundred workmen elected one delegate for every thousand employees. In the second election the delegates selected ten men to represent them in the Central War-Industry Committee.

decided to call a new meeting to take up the question of election. . . .

On September 11, there was a large meeting of workmen at the Lessner factory to discuss the question of participation in the Central War-Industry Committee. Police appeared and asked the workmen to leave, but no attention was paid and the meeting continued. It passed a resolution, emphasizing the need of utilizing the election campaign to organize labour on a large scale and demand the calling of a labour congress to decide whether the workmen should participate in the War-Industry Committee. . . .

In connection with the election of representatives of labour to the Central War-Industry Committee and the need of having free pre-election meetings, chairman A. I. Guchkov and vice-chairman A. I. Konovalov, of the Central War-Industry Committee, called on Prince N. B. Scherbatov, Minister of the Interior. They impressed upon him the importance of having free elections so as to interest the workmen of the capital in the great work. Guchkov also went to see General Frolov, the chief of the Petrograd Military District, while Konovalov called on Prince Obolenski, the head of the Petrograd police.

All the above-named representatives of the Government said that they would place no obstacles to the election of such delegates. On September 14, Konovalov and M. S. Margulies went to see Prince Shakhovskoi, the Minister of Commerce and Industry, and asked him to issue instructions along that line to the factory inspectors, which he promised to do.

It was intended to ask all government factories to take part in the election. With that in mind, Konovalov went to the Ministries of War and Navy and to the Red Cross to ask that elections be permitted in their institutions. . . .

The Central War-Industry Committee sent 1,130,000 notices to the different factories, calling upon the workmen to unite with the public organizations to drive off the foe, notifying them that the authorities had been asked to keep the police and inspectors from interfering in the pre-election assemblies and the elections, and requesting the owners of factories to assist the workmen in every possible way, provide them with halls, etc. for discussion and election. . . .

In many factories there were large, orderly meetings, at which labour decided to take part in the election. The workmen made some changes in the electoral system suggested by the War-Industry Committee. They [the workmen] proposed that commissions should be selected in every factory to count votes, to take up with the city authorities matters relating to the elections, etc. Workmen attach much importance to these commissions, hoping that they may become permanent bodies and occupy themselves with the welfare of the workers, cost of living, improvement in labour conditions, etc. . . . At pre-election meetings, it was agreed to name candidates, one for every thousand workmen. . . . It is likely that the number of men chosen will be greater than that supposed by the War-Industry Committee. . . .

The appeal of the Central War-Industry Committee to the workmen to participate in the mobilization of industry became the most discussed question in all the large Petrograd factories. The original plan of some groups, to elect workmen to the Central War-Industry Committees, did not meet with much response in Labour circles. Several pre-election meetings of workmen had already taken place and the question was thoroughly discussed.

At the 'Novyi Lessner' factory there was a large pre-election meeting on September 25. The management set aside one of its large shops for this purpose, erected a tribune for the speakers, and placed a table for the chairman. In short, it offered the workmen opportunities that they had not enjoyed for a long time. Representatives of the Bolsheviks, Mensheviks, and Narodniks made speeches.

The meeting did not end without differences of opinion. It was decided to name a factory commission to count votes, prepare for the election, etc. . . .

It became clear immediately that there would be two tickets: one of the Mensheviks and Narodniks combined, and the other of the Bolsheviks. The majority voted for the combined ticket. Before voting, it was proposed that the three parties be given an equal number of candidates and all go on the same ticket, but the Bolsheviks declined. Consequently, the commission of twenty-six persons elected were made up of Mensheviks and Narodniks. The next question taken up was the selection of a committee of five to prepare for the election of representatives to the War-Industry Committee. There was no agreement even on this point.

At the time of selecting the committee, which will take place on October 5, two tickets will be put in the field. When some people present expressed their discontent with the way the political groups were acting, the Bolsheviks left the hall. The meeting lasted five hours, and the workers of the two shifts took part.

(Frank Golder, *Documents of Russian History 1914–1917*, trans. Emanuel Aronsberg, Century, 1927)

II.9 'Resolution of the conference on the high cost of living' (24–26 July 1915)

[Representatives of the Union of Cities, co-operatives, labour organizations, public organizations, and learned professions were present at this Russian conference. It was the first meeting of its kind after the outbreak of the war and the first opportunity for the expression of public opinion.]

The year of the war has put the country to a great test. The results achieved and the great sacrifices offered show that the brave Russian army was not sufficiently equipped with fighting material. The necessary measures for providing the needed supplies were not taken in time by the organs of the Government, which are not responsible to the country.

The great effort and sacrifice of our army is made more difficult by the internal disorganization of the food supply, trade, and transport. The army and the civilian population are ready to make sacrifices and to undergo hardships to defend the country and to conquer the enemy who has crossed our border.

At the opening of the war all the elements of the population, conscious of their historic duty to the country and her future, united in the struggle for victory. But this burst of enthusiasm and popular exertion found no way of expressing itself.

The expectation that there would be a transformation in the organs of Government was not realized.

1. In order to succeed in the fight it is necessary to bring together all the forces of the land and to adapt, as quickly as possible, the whole life of the country to a state of war.

2. In this time of danger, an act to conciliate and to forget the old political fight would arouse the spirit of the population and would bring back to work and to public service many citizens who, for political reasons, have been kept away.

3. With the view of uniting all the forces of the country, an end should be put to the legal differences that exist between the different religions and nationalities in Russia.

4. For the same reason and in order to fight effectively against the high cost of living, as well as to provide steady and better conditions of employment in factories and mills, it is necessary to permit at once the free organization of labour, and to grant freedom of speech and the press.

5. Without taking into consideration the different forms of popular representation which are proposed by the various political groups and parties, the Conference agrees that at the present time, for the successful carrying on of the war, the Government should at least be made up of persons who have the confidence of the country. Only such men will make the Government strong, vigorous, capable of carrying this great country to victory.

(Frank Golder, *Documents of Russian History 1914–1917*, trans. Emanuel Aronsberg, Century, 1927)

II.10 Dragolioub Yovanovitch, from *The Economic and Social Effects of the War in Serbia* (1929)

During the war, the peasants enlarged their horizons. Their needs developed. The women in particular changed greatly. More and more they abandoned national costume. The men too showed a certain tendency in this direction, but to a lesser extent than the women. They tended simply to adopt one element or another of European costume: a hat, waistcoat or even shoes, or even all three, but they did not generally go very far, or else they changed by stages. radical, particularly the young ones. Nowadays the on fete days one cannot find a single young peasant girl woman in national costume. In the course of their moveme place to another during the terrible years, country people learne great distances, and to make use of other means of transport than legs or their oxen carts. Where these exist (West Serbia) both the male a female peasant now readily take both train and motorbus.

The peasants also learned to read newspapers. Before the war, reading a newspaper was a matter for shame: it was 'fine for gentlemen; the peasant should concentrate on his work'. The war put newspapers into the hands of the peasant, in the same way that military service introduced him to a proper bed. He would still be unlikely to read a book, still less a review. But newspapers have become familiar to him. It still seems to be impossible for him to make a regular order with regular payments, but he likes to read a newspaper from time to time. Nowadays one frequently sees a peasant woman buying a newspaper and taking it home: something quite impossible to imagine before the war.

It makes one sad to say it, but this does appear to be a truth: in the backward countries, general mobilization and war are almost the only ways of dragging them out of their old ways and inspiring change in the uncountable masses who constitute the majority of the population, of revealing in them producers who know how to work and consumers who have superior needs. But, in spite of all the individual and collective progress realized by the war to the profit of those who survived, the latter would under no circumstances wish to repeat the experience. Let us hope that future generations will find other methods for resolving their difficulties and pressing forward the chariot of progress!

(*Les effets économiques et sociaux de la guerre en Serbie*, New York, Carnegie Endowment, 1929, pp. 314–15)

II.11   Entries from the journal of Brand Whitlock (1916)

August 12, 1916. – The Kelloggs here for the week-end. Kellogg's interview with von Gersky this afternoon was, I take it, somewhat reassuring.

I hear, and there seems to be no doubt of it, that Sir Roger Casement has been hanged. While technically, and from the legal standpoint, this may have been right, the action of England in reference to the whole Irish revolution is one of the most disheartening things in the present disheartening condition of the world. Waiving the question for the moment of the whole English treatment of Ireland, and it has been a series of cruel, wanton, ignorant blunders for eight centuries, one might have expected a nobler attitude from that England that pretends to be fighting, and in a way is fighting, for civilization and the liberation of mankind; one might have expected some mercy from enlightened men for misguided and

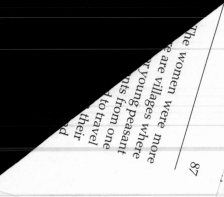

ɾ Ireland! But poorer England, far
ɩerous action. Think what Lincoln
ɩcy! But there are, alas, no Lincolns in
ɾ chancelleries, indeed!

ɩve organized a *centrale* to distribute the
ɩore butter to be had. They have fixed a
the French Revolution, just as in every
ɩg has been tried – the laws of economics
ɩn the laws of men – there is no butter for
the human intelligence, so-called, never

reliance on law, statistics, and so on. The
Germans ɪ̣̣.   ̦s in Flanders, based on the number of hens
according to their reɔ   ɩsus. So many hens, so many eggs! Poor hens!
They will have to hustle to keep out of the Kommandantur. And the
pigeons! They may fly out at a certain hour, but must be back in their cotes
at a given time!

August 15, 1916. – Francqui brought to our attention several letters from
the Governor-General of a similar character. The Comité National gives
relief to wives of Belgian officers. One woman, however, had had a baby
by a German officer; and the Comité National suppressed her relief. The
Governor-General rudely demanded that it be restored! There are several
cases of this sort.

August 17, 1916. – One of the curious things the war has brought to
Belgium is a certain liberation of women. They go out alone without
chaperons; some of them walk among the poor side streets, and so forth,
which many of them had never seen before. Girls ride everywhere on
bicycles, there being no automobiles or other form of transport. Van
Holder [a well-known painter in Brussels] says girls come and pose at his
studio for their portraits; girls of the best families, without a chaperon, as
they never did before the war. And Count de Jonghe made a similar
observation to me the other day. Women seem to have found themselves;
they *work*, from patriotic motives, but they work.

August 18, 1916. – A placard today announced that meat can be used, I
think, only twice a week in restaurants, or that only one *plat* can be served
at a meal; that cream must not be used at all, and so on. It is the beginning
of the tightening of the screws – and of the belt, too. The winter will be
very terrible.

(*The Letters and Journal of Brand Whitlock*, ed. Allan Nevins, East Norwalk,
Conn., Appleton-Century, 1936, pp. 286–7)

II.12 Report on British servants, *Bristol Evening News* (19 Feb. 1919)

CALL OF THE HOME UNHEEDED BY MANY GIRLS – BRISTOL SCHEME TO SOLVE PROBLEM

A meeting of employers and mistresses, arranged by the Local Advisory Committee, was held yesterday in the lesser Colston Hall, in regard to the question of domestic service in Bristol. Miss B. M. Sparks explained in opening the meeting, that it was imperative that some scheme should be evolved by which girls should be brought back to work in the homes, and to do this the conditions of domestic service must be brought into line with those of other industries, both in regarding details of conditions and wages. A draft scheme had been drawn up by the Women's Sub-Committee of the Local Advisory Committee, and it would be explained by Mr Broad, and suggestions regarding the scheme were invited.

Miss Baron pointed out that the subject was the most pressing among those affecting women's work. Women coming out of munitions indus-tries who were in domestic service before the war showed no inclination to go back into service. That was not only the case in Bristol but all over the country, and Local Advisory Committees set up in connection with Employment Exchanges to deal with employment questions were finding everywhere that this question was most pressing. The girls' point of view must be regarded as well as the employers'. The girls had an opportunity of doing another kind of work during the war. They had more freedom, definite hours of work, and more companionship in their work. They had also felt that every bit of their work was tremendously worthwhile doing and helped in the war. They did not want to give up their freedom and companionship, or the better status they had enjoyed. To give an idea of what was happening in Bristol; there were something like 1,900 unem-ployed claiming donations at present, a large number of whom were probably in domestic service before the war. The Exchange had been inundated with vacancies since the meeting of domestic workers about a fortnight ago. There were 400 vacancies at present for domestics to live in, and 150 for daily workers. To show how few girls were going back to domestic service, during the four weeks ended February 7, nineteen women were placed to live in and 53 daily workers. It seemed as if something must be done to change the conditions and make domestic service more attractive. Long hours and lack of freedom were the chief objections. Various schemes had been drawn up by various bodies, one of which provided for the girls to live together in a hostel and wear a special uniform, and be under a certain amount of discipline.

Mr L. Broad [outlined] the scheme which was suggested for Bristol . . . (A 'Whitley' council representing employers and employed was to be constituted and from it a rota to vet prospective domestics and mistresses.)

Wages and hours. The following minimum wages would apply for resident domestics: Cooks, 21 years and upwards £30; house parlour-maids, parlourmaids and housemaids, 18 years £22, 19 years £24, 20 years £26, 21 years and upwards, £28. Generals; 18 years £20, 19 years £22, 20 years £24, 21 years and upwards £26. Between maids; 18 years £15, 19 years £20. These wages were in addition to full board and washing. The women would be given two hours daily, irrespective of meal times, a half-day holiday every week, a half-day on Sundays, and two weeks holiday a year on full wages. For meal times they would have half-hour for breakfast, one hour for dinner, and half-hour for tea. Employers would be asked to sign an agreement on these conditions, and give an assurance that the situation was a good and comfortable one, and the sleeping accommodation was satisfactory. There would be a month's notice on either side. Any complaint as to conditions of service should be referred to the weekly rota. With regard to daily and part-time workers, general work with meals would be 4d per hour (exclusive of meal times) and 6d without meals.

Criticism of the scheme was invited, and there was some discussion of details. Replying to a question as to this scheme having the effect of raising the wages of girls at present employed at lower rates, Mr Broad said the scheme might have that effect. . . . One lady thought such conditions would make the girl more the mistress than the employer herself. . . .

(*Bristol Evening News*, 19 Feb. 1919)

II.13   Wilfred Owen, 'Strange meeting' (1918)

PREFACE

This book is not about heroes. English poetry is not yet fit to speak of them.

Nor is it about deeds, or lands, nor anything about glory, honour, might, majesty, dominion, or power, except War.

Above all I am not concerned with Poetry.

My subject is War, and the pity of War.

The Poetry is in the pity.

Yet these elegies are to this generation in no sense consolatory. They may be to the next. All a poet can do today is warn. That is why the true Poets must be truthful.

(If I thought the letter of this book would last, I might have used proper names; but if the spirit of it survives – survives Prussia – my ambition and those names will have achieved themselves fresher fields than Flanders. . . .)

STRANGE MEETING

It seemed that out of battle I escaped
Down some profound dull tunnel, long since scooped
Through granites which titanic wars had groined.
Yet also there encumbered sleepers groaned,
Too fast in thought or death to be bestirred.
Then, as I probed them, one sprang up, and stared
With piteous recognition in fixed eyes,
Lifting distressful hands as if to bless.
And by his smile, I knew that sullen hall,
By his dead smile I knew we stood in Hell.
With a thousand pains that vision's face was grained;
Yet no blood reached there from the upper ground,
And no guns thumped, or down the flues made moan.
'Strange friend,' I said, 'here is no cause to mourn.'
'None,' said that other, 'save the undone years,
The hopelessness. Whatever hope is yours,
Was my life also; I went hunting wild
After the wildest beauty in the world,
Which lies not calm in eyes, or braided hair,
But mocks the steady running of the hour,
And if it grieves, grieves richlier than here.
For of my glee might many men have laughed,
And of my weeping something had been left,
Which must die now. I mean the truth untold.
The pity of war, the pity war distilled.
Now men will go content with what we spoiled,
Or, discontent, boil bloody, and be spilled.
They will be swift with swiftness of the tigress.
None will break ranks, though nations trek from progress.
Courage was mine, and I had mystery,
Wisdom was mine, and I had mastery:
To miss the march of this retreating world
Into vain citadels that are not walled.
Then, when much blood had clogged their chariot-wheels,
I would go up and wash them from sweet wells,
Even with truths that lie too deep for taint.
I would have poured my spirit without stint
But not through wounds; not on the cess of war.
Foreheads of men have bled where no wounds were.
I am the enemy you killed, my friend.
I knew you in this dark: for so you frowned
Yesterday through me as you jabbed and killed.
I parried; but my hands were loath and cold.
Let us sleep now. . . .'

(*Wilfred Owen, Collected Poems*, Chatto and Windus, 1920)

II.14   Henri Barbusse, from *Under Fire* (1915)

'There are those who say,' now cries one of the sombre and compelling talkers, extending his hand as though he could see the pageant, 'there are those who say, "How fine they are!"'

'And those who say, "The nations hate each other!"'

'And those who say, "I get fat on war, and my belly matures on it!"'

'And those who say, "There has always been war, so there always will be!"'

'There are those who say, "I can't see farther than the end of my nose, and I forbid others to see farther!"'

'There are those who say, "Babies come into the world with either red or blue breeches on!"'

'There are those,' growled a hoarse voice, 'who say, "Bow your head and trust in God!"'

◆　◆　◆

Ah, you are right, poor countless workmen of the battles, you who have made with your hands all of the Great War, you whose omnipotence is not yet used for well-doing, you human host whose every face is a world of sorrows, you who dream bowed under the yoke of a thought beneath that sky where long black clouds rend themselves and expand in dishevelled lengths like evil angels – yes, you are right. There are all those things against you. Against you and your great common interests, which are precisely and with sacred logic blended, there are not only the sword-wavers, the profiteers, and the intriguers.

There is not only the prodigious opposition of interested parties – financiers, speculators great and small, armour-plated in their banks and houses, who live on war and live in peace during war, with their brows stubbornly set upon a secret doctrine and their faces shut up like safes.

There are those who admire the exchange of flashing blows, who hail like women the bright colours of uniforms; those whom military music and the martial ballads poured upon the public intoxicate as with brandy; the dizzy-brained, the feeble-minded, the superstitious, the savages.

There are those who bury themselves in the past, on whose lips are the sayings only of bygone days, the traditionalists for whom an injustice has legal force because it is perpetuated, who aspire to be guided by the dead, who strive to subordinate progress and the future and all their palpitating passion to the realm of ghosts and nursery-tales.

With them are all the parsons, who seek to excite you and to lull you to sleep with the morphine of their Paradise, so that nothing may change.

They pervert the most admirable of moral principles. How many are the crimes of which they have made virtues merely by dowering them with the word 'national'? They distort even truth itself. For the truth which is eternally the same they substitute each their national truth. So many nations, so many truths; and thus they falsify and twist the truth. All those people are your enemies.

They are your enemies as much as those German soldiers are to-day who are prostrate here between you in the mud, who are only poor dupes hatefully deceived and brutalised, domestic beasts. They are your enemies, wherever they were born, however they pronounce their names, whatever the language in which they lie. Look at them, in the heaven and on the earth. Look at them, everywhere! Identify them once for all, and be mindful for ever!

♦ ♦ ♦

'They will say to you,' growled a kneeling man who stooped with his two hands in the earth and shook his shoulders like a mastiff, ' "My friend, you have been a wonderful hero!" I don't *want* them to say it!

'Heroes? Some sort of extraordinary being? Idols? Rot! We've been murderers. We have respectably followed the trade of murderers. We shall do it again with all our might, if we have to turn murderers again so that the real enemies can be left in peace. The act of slaughter is always ignoble; sometimes necessary, but always ignoble. Yes, hard and persistent murderers, that's what we've been. But don't talk to me about military virtue because I've killed Germans.'

'Nor to me,' cried another in so loud a voice that no one could have replied to him even had he dared; 'nor to me, because I've saved the lives of Frenchmen! Why, we might as well set fire to houses for the sake of the excellence of life-saving!'

'It would be a crime to exhibit the fine side of war, even if there were one!' murmured one of the sombre soldiers.

The first man continued. 'They'll say those things to us by way of paying us with glory, and to pay themselves, too, for what they haven't done. But military glory – it isn't even true for us common soldiers. It's for some, but outside those elect the soldier's glory is a lie, like every other fine-looking thing in war. In reality, the soldier's sacrifice is obscurely concealed. The multitudes that make up the waves of attack have no reward. They run to hurl themselves into a frightful inglorious nothing. You cannot even heap up their names, their poor little names of nobodies.'

'To hell with it all,' replies a man, 'we've got other things to think about.'

'But all that,' hiccupped a face which the mud concealed like a hideous hand, 'may you even *say* it? You'd be cursed, and "shot at dawn"! They've made around a Marshal's plumes a religion as bad and stupid and malignant as the other!'

The man raised himself, fell down, and rose again. The wound that he had under his armour of filth was staining the ground, and when he had spoken, his wide-open eyes looked down at all the blood he had given for the healing of the world.

♦ ♦ ♦

The others, one by one, straighten themselves. The storm is falling more heavily on the expanse of flayed and martyred fields. The day is full of night. It is as if new hostile shapes of men and groups of men are rising unceasingly on the crest of the mountain-chain of clouds, round about the barbaric outlines of crosses, eagles, churches, royal and military palaces, temples and money-markets. They seem to multiply there, shutting out the stars that are fewer than mankind; it seems even as if these apparitions are moving in all directions in the excavated ground, here, there, among the real beings who are thrown there at random, half buried in the earth like grains of corn.

My still living companions have at last got up. Standing with difficulty on the foundered soil, enclosed in their bemired garb, laid out in strange upright coffins of mud, raising their huge simplicity out of the earth's depths – a profundity like that of ignorance – they move and cry out, with their gaze, their arms and their fists extended towards the sky whence fall daylight and storm. They are struggling against victorious spectres, like the Cyranos and Don Quixotes that they still are.

One sees their shadows stirring on the shining sad expanse of the plain, and reflected in the pallid stagnant surface of the old trenches, which now only the infinite void of space inhabits and purifies, in the centre of a polar desert whose horizons fume.

But their eyes are opened. They are beginning to make out the bound-less simplicity of things. And Truth not only invests them with a dawn of hope, but raises on it a renewal of strength and courage.

'That's enough talk about those others!' one of the men commanded; 'all the worse for them! – Us! Us all!' The understanding between democracies, the entente among the multitudes, the uplifting of the people of the world, the bluntly simple faith! All the rest, aye, all the rest, in the past, the present and the future, matters nothing at all.

And a soldier ventures to add this sentence, though he begins it with lowered voice, 'If the present war has advanced progress by one step, its miseries and slaughter will count for little.'

And while we get ready to rejoin the others and begin war again, the dark and storm-choked sky slowly opens above our heads. Between two masses of gloomy cloud a tranquil gleam emerges; and that line of light, so black-edged and beset, brings even so its proof that the sun is there.

(*Under Fire*, trans. W. Fitzwater-Wray, Dent, 1965, pp. 339–43)

II.15 Erich Maria Remarque, from *All Quiet on the Western Front* (1929)

It is autumn. There are not many of the old hands left. I am the last of the seven fellows from our class.

Everyone talks of peace and armistice. All wait. If it again proves an illusion, then they will break up; hope is high, it cannot be taken away again without an upheaval. If there is not peace, then there will be revolution.

I have fourteen days rest, because I have swallowed a bit of gas; in the little garden I sit the whole day long in the sun. The armistice is coming soon, I believe it now too. Then we will go home.

Here my thoughts stop and will not go any farther. All that meets me, all that floods over me are but feelings – greed of life, love of home, yearning for the blood, intoxication of deliverance. But no aims.

Had we returned home in 1916, out of the suffering and the strength of our experiences we might have unleashed a storm. Now if we go back we will be weary, broken, burnt out, rootless, and without hope. We will not be able to find our way any more.

And men will not understand us – for the generation that grew up before us, though it has passed these years with us already had a home and a calling; now it will return to its old occupations, and the war will be forgotten – and the generation that has grown up after us will be strange to us and push us aside. We will be superfluous even to ourselves, we will grow older, a few will adapt themselves, some others will merely submit, and most will be bewildered; – the years will pass by and in the end we shall fall into ruin.

But perhaps all this that I think is mere melancholy and dismay, which will fly away as the dust, when I stand once again beneath the poplars and listen to the rustling of their leaves. It cannot be that it has gone, the yearning that made our blood unquiet, the unknown, the perplexing, the oncoming things, the thousand faces of the future, the melodies from dreams and from books, the whispers and divinations of women; it cannot be that this has vanished in bombardment, in despair, in brothels.

Here the trees show gay and golden, the berries of the rowan stand red among the leaves, country roads run white out to the sky line, and the canteens hum like beehives with rumours of peace.

I stand up.

I am very quiet. Let the months and years come, they can take nothing from me, they can take nothing more. I am so alone, and so without hope that I can confront them without fear. The life that has borne me through these years is still in my hands and my eyes. Whether I have subdued it, I know not. But so long as it is there it will seek its own way out, heedless of the will that is within me. . . .

He fell in October 1918, on a day that was so quiet and still on the whole front, that the army report confined itself to the single sentence: All quiet on the Western Front.

He had fallen forward and lay on the earth as though sleeping. Turning him over one saw that he could not have suffered long; his face had an expression of calm, as though almost glad the end had come.

(*All Quiet on the Western Front*, trans. A. W. Wheen, Picador, 1987)

II.16 'The programme of the Progressive Bloc' (25 Aug. 1915)

The undersigned representatives of parties and groups in the State Council and in the State *Duma*, out of the conviction that only a strong, firm, and active authority can lead our fatherland to victory, and that such an authority can only be one supported by the confidence of the public and capable of organizing the active co-operation of all citizens, have come to the unanimous conclusion that the most essential and important task of creating such an authority cannot be realized without the fulfilment of the following conditions:

The formation of a united government, consisting of persons who enjoy the confidence of the country and are in agreement with the legislative institutions as to carrying out, at the earliest time, a definite programme; a decisive change in the methods of government hitherto employed, which have been founded on distrust of public initiative, in particular: (a) strict observance of the principle of legality in administration; (b) removal of the dual power of military and civil authority in questions that have no immediate relation to the conduct of military operations; (c) renovation of the personnel of local administration; (d) an intelligent and consistent policy directed to the maintenance of internal peace and the removal of discord between nationalities and classes.

For the realization of such a policy, the following measures must be taken in both the administrative and the legislative systems:

1. By amnesty from the Sovereign, the withdrawal of cases initiated on charges of purely political and religious offences which are not complicated by offences of a criminal character; the remission of punishment and restoration of rights, including that of taking part in elections to the State *Duma*, to *zemstvo* and town institutions, and so on, for persons condemned for such offences, and some mitigation for others who have been condemned for political and religious offences, with the exception of spies and traitors.

2. The return of those administratively exiled for offences of a political character.

3. Full and decisive cessation of persecution for religion under any pretext whatsoever, and repeal of circulars limiting and distorting the meaning of the decree of April 17, 1905 [on religious tolerance].

4. A settlement of the Russo-Polish question, that is: repeal of limitations on the rights of Poles all over Russia, the immediate preparation and introduction into the legislative institutions of a bill on the autonomy of Russian Poland, and the simultaneous revision of the laws on Polish land ownership.

5. A beginning towards abolishing the limitations on the rights of Jews, in particular, further steps for the abolition of the Jewish Pale, facilitation

of access to educational institutions, and a repeal of limitations on the choice of a profession; the restoration of the Jewish press.

6. A policy of conciliation in the Finnish question – in particular, a change in the personnel of the administration and the Senate, and the cessation of persecution of officials.

7. Restoration of the Little Russian press; the immediate review of the cases of inhabitants of Galicia kept under arrest or exiled, and the liberation of those of them who, though innocent, were subjected to prosecution.

8. The restoration of the work of trade unions, and cessation of persecution of the workers' representatives in sick benefit funds, on suspicion of belonging to an illegal party; restoration of the labour press.

9. Agreement between the government and the legislative institutions as to the speediest introduction of:

(a) All bills that are most closely related to national defence, the supplying of the army, the care of the wounded, the regulation of the lot of refugees, and other problems directly connected with the war.

(b) The following programme of legislative work, directed towards organizing the country to contribute to victory and towards the maintenance of internal peace: equalization of the rights of peasants with those of other classes; the introduction of *volost' zemstvos*; the revision of the *zemstvo* law of 1890; the revision of the municipal law of 1892; the introduction of *zemstvo* institutions in outlying areas, such as Siberia, the Archangel *guberniia* [provinces], the Don region, the Caucasus, and so on; bills on co-operative societies, on rest days for shop assistants, on improving the lot of postal and telegraph employees, on approving temperance forever, on *zemstvo* and town congresses and unions, on the statute concerning inspections, and on the introduction of justices of the peace in those *guberniias* where their introduction has been halted for financial reasons; and the carrying out of such legislative measures as may be found to be necessary for the administrative execution of the above-described programme of action.

Signed:
For the Progressive Nationalist Group,
     V. A. Bobrinskii
For the Centre Faction,
     V. N. L'vov
For the Zemstvo-Octobrist Faction,
     I. I. Dmitriukov
For the Union of 17 October Group,
     S. I. Shidlovskii
For the Progressivist Faction,
     I. N. Efremov
For the People's Freedom [Kadet] Faction,
     P. N. Miliukov

For the Academic Group of the State Council,
    D. D. Grimm
For the Centre Group of the State Council,
    Baron V. Meller-Zakomel'skii

(George Vernadsky *et al.* (eds) *A Source Book for Russian History from Early Times to 1917*, New Haven, Conn., Yale University Press, 1972, vol. 3, pp. 846–7)

II.17 Paul Miliukov, extracts from a speech in the *Duma* (1 Nov. 1916)

[Paul Miliukov was a leader of the Kadet Party.]

As heretofore, we are striving for complete victory; as heretofore, we are prepared to make all the necessary sacrifices; and, as heretofore, we are anxious to preserve our national unity. But I say this candidly: there is a difference in the situation. We have lost faith in the ability of this government to achieve victory (*Voices*: 'That's true'), because, as far as this government is concerned, neither the attempts at correction nor the attempts at improvement which we have made here have proved successful. All the Allied Powers have summoned to the ranks of their governments the very best men of all parties. They have gathered about the heads of their governments all the confidence and all those elements of organization present in their countries, which are better organized than our own. What has our own government accomplished? Our [Progressive Bloc] declaration has told that. When there was formed in the Fourth State *Duma* a majority [the Progressive Bloc] which the *Duma* had lacked theretofore, a majority ready to vote its confidence in a cabinet worthy of such confidence, then nearly all those men who might in some slight degree have been expected to receive such confidence were forced, systematically, one after another, every one of them, to leave the cabinet. And if we have formerly said that our government had neither the knowledge nor the talent necessary for the present moment, we say now, gentlemen, that this present government has sunk beneath the level on which it stood during normal times in Russian life. (*Voices on the Left*: 'True! Right!') And now the gulf between us and that government has grown wider and has become impassable.

Today we see and are aware that with this government we cannot legislate, any more than we can with this government lead Russia to victory . . . We are telling this government, as the declaration of the Bloc stated: We shall fight you; we shall fight with all legitimate means until you go. . . . When the *Duma* with ever greater persistence insists that the rear must be organized for a successful struggle, while the government persists in claiming that organizing the country means organizing a revolution and deliberately prefers chaos and disorganization, then what is this: stupidity or treason? (*A voice on the Left*: 'Treason!' *Adzhemov*: 'Stupidity!' *Laughter*.) . . .

You must realize, also, why we, too, have no task left to us today other than that which I have already pointed out: to obtain the resignation of this government . . . We have many, very many, separate reasons for being dissatisfied with the government. If we have time, we shall speak of them. But all these particular reasons boil down to this general one: the government, as presently composed, is incapable and ill intentioned. (*Voices on the Left*: 'Correct!') This is the main evil, a victory over which will be tantamount to winning the whole campaign.

(George Vernadsky *et al.* (eds) *A Source Book for Russian History from Early Times to 1917*, New Haven, Conn., Yale University Press, 1972, vol. 3, p. 870)

II.18 Nicholai Markov, extract from a speech in the *Duma* (3 Nov. 1916)

[Markov was a member of the right-wing Union of the Russian People.]

If the people and the workers believe your words . . . then . . . be aware that the people and the workers are men of action, men with toil-hardened hands; they are not windbags, and, unfortunately, they do believe your words; and if you say 'we shall fight against government authority during this terrible war,' then realize that this means that the workers would strike, that they would raise the banner of revolt; and do not hide behind the pretence that you wish to confine yourself to words alone. No, be aware that your words will lead to revolt, to rebellion, to an insurrection of the people, to a weakening of the state at a time when the state is trembling from the blows of a hateful, evil, despicable enemy.

Gentlemen, you apparently do not realize what you wish to accomplish, so I shall explain it to you: you wish to bring on a revolution in Russia so that a revolution would destroy the entire Russian state, well formed or not.

(George Vernadsky *et al.* (eds) *A Source Book for Russian History from Early Times to 1917*, New Haven, Conn., Yale University Press, 1972, vol. 3, pp. 870–1)

II.19 Vladimir Purishkevich, extract from a speech in the *Duma* (19 Nov. 1916)

[Purishkevich was founder of the Union of the Russian People.]

Gentlemen, I mount this tribune today with inexpressible emotional agitation, and not because I have left the ranks of my faction. I cannot abandon the ranks of the Right, for I am perhaps the Right-most of all those who are in the Right camp. But there are moments, gentlemen . . .

when one cannot allow oneself to speak from the bell tower of an *uezd* or *guberniia* town but must ring the alarm from the bell tower of Ivan the Great [in the Kremlin in Moscow] . . . Today, as formerly and in the future, there burns within me an infinite love for my native land and a selfless, boundless, and most devoted allegiance to my sovereign. I am living at this moment with but a single thought – that of a Russian victory. But today, as before, I have within me no slavish obsequiousness before the organs of the ruling power, and I could not enter my name as a member of the ministerial antechamber. (*Applause in the Centre and on the Left. Voices in the Centre*: 'Bravo!') I clearly see, gentlemen, who and what it is that is harming Russia, impeding her, and postponing the hour of her certain victory over the external enemy.

The disorganization of our rear is undoubtedly being carried out by the enemy, and it is being done by a strong, relentless, and resolute hand. We have a single system, the system of devastation in the rear. This system was set up by Wilhelm himself and is being carried out by him with amazing consistency with the aid of the German party working in our rear.

What today, gentlemen, is the principal scourge of Russian public and official life? Here are four propositions: the first is the senseless censorship of that which ought not to be censored; the second is the hypocrisy and paralysis of the government; the third is the dangerous symptoms of the triumph of Germanophile tendencies among the organs of the government; and, in connection with this, the fourth is absolute uncertainty as to the morrow, with new government policies cooked up from day to day.

I take the liberty to say here, from the rostrum of the State *Duma*, that all this evil comes from those dark forces, from those influences which push this or that individual into position and which force up into high posts people who are not capable of filling them, from those influences headed by Grishka Rasputin . . . It is necessary that the legislative body, being the voice of the entire country and now united in spirit on the question of victory, finally raise its voice about this, Russia's greatest evil, which is corrupting Russian public life. These past nights I couldn't sleep, I give you my word of honour. I lie with eyes open and imagine a series of telegrams, reports, notes which this illiterate peasant writes now to one minister, then to another, and most frequently of all, it is said, to Aleksandr Dmitrievich Protopopov,* and which he requests them to act upon. And we know there were instances when the failure to fulfil these demands entailed the fall of these strong and powerful men. . . .

I shall take the liberty of addressing now the Council of Ministers, quite apart from the *Duma*, whose duty I have already indicated. If the

---

* Protopopov was the last tzarist minister of the interior appointed in September 1916 on the insistence of the Tzarina and on the advice of Rasputin. Protopopov was believed to have made peace overtures to Germany.

ministers consider duty above career – and I believe that at this moment duty is above career – and if you really are a united cabinet, then go to the tsar and say that things cannot go on any longer in this way. This is not a boycott of authority, gentlemen, but your duty before the sovereign. If you are loyal to your sovereign, if the glory of Russia, her power, her future, intimately and inseparably bound up with the grandeur and splendour of the tsar's name, are dear to you, go to Imperial Headquarters, throw yourselves at the tsar's feet, and beg permission to open his eyes to the dreadful reality, beg him to deliver Russia from Rasputin and the Rasputinites both big and small. . . .

Gentlemen, we must plead with the sovereign, and you (*turning to the ministers*), his loyal servants, chosen to carry out his will, you, primarily responsible for the course of the Russian ship of state, united with us, go to headquarters and plead with the sovereign that Grishka Rasputin not be the leader of Russian internal public life. (*Loud and prolonged applause from the Centre, Left, and Right; voices*: 'Bravo!')

(George Vernadsky *et al.* (eds) *A Source Book for Russian History from Early Times to 1917*, New Haven, Conn., Yale University Press, 1972, vol. 3, pp. 872–3)

II.20 'The Proclamation of the Provisional Government' (1 March 1917)

FROM THE PROVISIONAL GOVERNMENT

Citizens!

The Provisional Committee of members of the State *Duma*, with the aid and sympathy of the troops and the population of the capital, has at present scored such a degree of success over the dark forces of the old regime that it can now proceed to a more durable organization of executive power.

To this end, the Provisional Committee of the State *Duma* appoints as ministers of the first public [*obshchestvennyi*] cabinet the following persons, the country's confidence in whom is guaranteed by their past public and political activities.

Chairman of the Council of Ministers and Minister of Internal Affairs: Prince G. E. L'vov

Minister of Foreign Affairs: P. N. Miliukov

Minister of War and the Navy: A. I. Guchkov

Minister of Means of Communications: N. V. Nekrasov

Minister of Trade and Industry: A. I. Konovalov

Minister of Public Education: A. A. Manuilov

Minister of Finance: M. I. Tereshchenko

Chief Procurator of the Holy Synod: V. N. L'vov

Minister of Agriculture: A. I. Shingarev

Minister of Justice: A. F. Kerenskii

State Comptroller: I. V. Godnev

Minister for Finnish Affairs: F. I. Rodichev

The Cabinet will be guided in its present activity by the following principles:

1. Full and immediate amnesty in all political and religious cases, including terrorist attempts, military uprisings and agrarian offences, and so forth.

2. Freedom of speech, the press, unions, assembly, and strikes, with the extension of political freedoms to servicemen within limits permitted by military and technical conditions.

3. Abolition of all class, religious, and national restrictions.

4. Immediate preparations for the convocation – on the basis of universal, equal, direct, and secret suffrage – of a constituent assembly which will establish the form of government and the constitution of the country.

5. Replacement of the police by a people's militia with an elected command, subordinate to the organs of local self-government.

6. Elections to the organs of local self-government on the basis of universal, direct, equal, and secret ballot.

7. Non-disarmament and non-transfer from Petrograd of the military units that participated in the revolutionary movement.

8. Along with the preservation of strict military discipline in the ranks and during performance of military duty, the abolition of all restrictions upon the soldiers' enjoyment of those public rights that have been granted to all other citizens. The Provisional Government considers it its duty to add that it by no means intends to use the military situation to delay in any way the realization of the above reforms and measures.

Chairman of the State *Duma* M. V. Rodzianko

Chairman of the Council of Ministers Prince G. E. L'vov

Ministers: P. N. Miliukov, N. V. Nekrasov, A. I. Konovalov, A. A. Manuilov, M. I. Tereshchenko, Vl. N. L'vov, A. I. Shingarev, A. F. Kerenskii

(George Vernadsky *et al.* (eds) *A Source Book for Russian History from Early Times to 1917*, New Haven, Conn., Yale University Press, 1972, vol. 3, pp. 881–2)

II.21 'Order No 1' (1 March 1917)

To the garrison of the Petrograd *okrug*, to all the soldiers of the guard, army, artillery, and navy, for immediate and strict execution, and to the workers of Petrograd for their information:

The Soviet of Workers' and Soldiers' Deputies has resolved:

1. In all companies, battalions, regiments, parks, batteries, squadrons, in the special services of the various military administrations, and on the

vessels of the navy, committees of elected representatives from the lower ranks of the above-mentioned military units shall be chosen immediately.

2. In all those military units that have not yet chosen their representatives to the Soviet of Workers' Deputies, one representative from each company shall be selected, to report with written credentials at the building of the State *Duma* by ten o'clock in the morning of the third of this March.

3. In all its political activities the military branch is subordinated to the Soviet of Workers' and Soldiers' Deputies and to its own committees.

4. The orders of the military commission of the State *Duma* shall be executed only in such cases as they do not conflict with the orders and resolutions of the Soviet of Workers' and Soldiers' Deputies.

5. All kinds of arms, such as rifles, machine guns, armoured automobiles and others, must be kept at the disposal and under the control of the company and battalion committees and must in no case be turned over to officers, even at their demand.

6. In the ranks and during their performance of the duties of the service, soldiers must observe the strictest military discipline, but outside the service and the ranks, in their political, general civic, and private lives, soldiers cannot in any way be deprived of those rights that all citizens enjoy. In particular, standing at attention and compulsory saluting, when not on duty, are abolished.

7. Also, the addressing of the officers with the titles 'Your Excellency,' 'Your Honour,' and the like, is abolished, and these titles are replaced by the address of 'Mister General,' 'Mister Colonel,' and so forth. Rudeness towards soldiers of any rank, and, especially, addressing them as 'thou,' is prohibited, and soldiers are required to bring to the attention of the company committees every infraction of this rule, as well as all misunderstandings occurring between officers and enlisted men.

The present order is to be read to all companies, battalions, regiments, ships' crews, batteries, and other combatant and noncombatant commands.

The Petrograd Soviet of Workers' and
Soldiers' Deputies

(George Vernadsky *et al.* (eds) *A Source Book for Russian History from Early Times to 1917*, New Haven, Conn., Yale University Press, 1972, vol. 3, p. 882)

II.22 'Declaration of the Kronstadt soldiers' (1 March 1921)

Having heard the report of the representatives sent by the general meeting of ships' crews to Petrograd to investigate the situation there, we resolve:

1. In view of the fact that the present soviets do not express the will of the workers and peasants, immediately to hold new elections by secret ballot, with freedom to carry on agitation beforehand for all workers and peasants;

2. To give freedom of speech and press to workers and peasants, to anarchists and left socialist parties;

3. To secure freedom of assembly for trade unions and peasant organizations;

4. To call a non-party conference of the workers, Red Army soldiers, and sailors of Petrograd, Kronstadt, and Petrograd province, no later than March 10, 1921;

5. To liberate all political prisoners of socialist parties, as well as all workers, peasants, soldiers, and sailors imprisoned in connection with the labour and peasant movements;

6. To elect a commission to review the cases of those being held in prisons and concentration camps;

7. To abolish all political departments because no party should be given special privileges in the propagation of its ideas or receive the financial support of the state for such purposes. Instead, there should be established cultural and educational commissions, locally elected and financed by the state;

8. To remove immediately all roadblock detachments;

9. To equalize the rations of all working people, with the exception of those employed in trades detrimental to health;

10. To abolish the Communist fighting detachments in all branches of the army, as well as the Communist guards kept on duty in factories and mills. Should such guards or detachments be found necessary, they are to be appointed in the army from the ranks and in the factories and mills at the discretion of the workers;

11. To give the peasants full freedom of action in regard to the land, and also the right to keep cattle, on condition that the peasants manage with their own means, that is, without employing hired labour;

12. To request all branches of the army, as well as our comrades the military cadets (*kursanty*), to endorse our resolution;

13. To demand that the press give all our resolutions wide publicity;

14. To appoint an itinerant bureau of control;

15. To permit free handicrafts production by one's own labour.

PETRICHENKO, Chairman of the Squadron Meeting
PEREPELKIN, Secretary

(Paul Avrich, *Kronstadt 1921*, Princeton University Press, 1970, pp. 73–4)

II.23   'Kronstadt sailors' appeal' (8 March 1921)

WHAT WE ARE FIGHTING FOR

After carrying out the October Revolution, the working class had hoped to achieve its emancipation. But the result was an even greater enslavement of the human personality. The power of the police and gendarme monarchy passed into the hands of the Communist usurpers, who, instead of giving the people freedom, instilled in them the constant fear of falling into the torture chambers of the *Cheka*, which in their horrors far exceed the gendarme administration of the tsarist regime. The bayonets, bullets, and gruff commands of the *Cheka oprichniki* – these are what the working man of Soviet Russia has won after so much struggle and suffering. The glorious emblem of the workers' state – the sickle and hammer – has in fact been replaced by the Communist authorities with the bayonet and barred window, for the sake of maintaining the calm and carefree life of the new bureaucracy of Communist commissars and functionaries.

But most infamous and criminal of all is the moral servitude which the Communists have inaugurated: they have laid their hands also on the inner world of the toilers, forcing them to think in the Communist way. With the help of the bureaucratized trade unions, they have fastened the workers to their benches, so that labour has become not a joy but a new form of slavery. To the protests of the peasants, expressed in spontaneous uprisings, and those of the workers, whose living conditions have driven them out on strike, they answer with mass executions and bloodletting, in which they have not been surpassed even by the tsarist generals. Russia of the toilers, the first to raise the red banner of labour's emancipation, is drenched in the blood of those martyred for the glory of Communist domination. In this sea of blood, the Communists are drowning all the great and glowing pledges and watchwords of the workers' revolution. The picture has been drawn more and more sharply, and now it is clear that the Russian Communist party is not the defender of the toilers that it pretends to be. The interests of the working people are alien to it. Having gained power, it is afraid only of losing it, and therefore deems every means permissible: slander, violence, deceit, murder, vengeance upon the families of the rebels.

The long-suffering patience of the toilers is at an end. Here and there the land is lit up by the fires of insurrection in a struggle against oppression and violence. Strikes by the workers have flared up, but the Bolshevik *okhrana* agents have not been asleep and have taken every measure to forestall and suppress the inevitable third revolution. But it has come nevertheless, and it is being made by the hands of the toilers themselves. The generals of Communism see clearly that it is the people who have risen, convinced that the ideas of socialism have been betrayed. Yet, trembling for their skins and aware that there is no escape from the wrath of the workers, they still try, with the help of their *oprichniki*, to terrorize the rebels with prison, firing-squads, and other atrocities. But life under the yoke of the Communist dictatorship has become more terrible than death.

The rebellious working people understand that there is no middle ground in the struggle against the Communists and the new serfdom that they have erected. One must go on to the end. They give the appearance of making concessions: in Petrograd province roadblock detachments have been removed and 10 million gold rubles have been allotted for the purchase of foodstuffs from abroad. But one must not be deceived, for behind this bait is concealed the iron hand of the master, the dictator, who aims to be repaid a hundred-fold for his concessions once calm is restored.

No, there can be no middle ground. Victory or death! The example is being set by Red Kronstadt, menace of counterrevolutionaries of the right and of the left. Here the new revolutionary step forward has been taken. Here is raised the banner of rebellion against the three-year-old violence and oppression of Communist rule, which has put in the shade the three-hundred-year yoke of monarchism. Here in Kronstadt has been laid the first stone of the third revolution, striking the last fetters from the labouring masses and opening a broad new road for socialist creativity.

The new revolution will also rouse the labouring masses of the East and of the West, by serving as an example of the new socialist construction as opposed to the bureaucratic Communist 'creativity'. The labouring masses abroad will see with their own eyes that everything created here until now by the will of the workers and peasants was not socialism. Without a single shot, without a drop of blood, the first step has been taken. The toilers do not need blood. They will shed it only at a moment of self-defence. In spite of all the outrageous acts of the Communists, we have enough restraint to confine ourselves only to isolating them from public life so that their malicious and false agitation will not hinder our revolutionary work.

The workers and peasants steadfastly march forward, leaving behind them the Constituent Assembly, with its bourgeois regime, and the dictatorship of the Communist party, with its *Cheka* and its state capitalism, whose hangman's noose encircles the necks of the labouring masses and threatens to strangle them to death. The present overturn at last gives the toilers the opportunity to have their freely elected soviets, operating without the slightest force of party pressure, and to remark the bureaucratized trade unions into free associations of workers, peasants, and the labouring intelligentsia. At last the policeman's club of the Communist autocracy has been broken.

(Paul Avrich, *Kronstadt 1921*, Princeton University Press, 1970, pp. 241–3)

II.24 'The *Reichstag* Resolution of 19 July 1917'

The *Reichstag* strives for a peace of understanding and the permanent reconciliation of peoples. Forced territorial acquisitions and political, economic, or financial oppressions are irreconcilable with such a peace. The *Reichstag* also rejects all plans which aim at economic isolation and hostility among nations after the war. The freedom of the seas must be made secure. Only an economic peace will prepare the ground for a friendly intercourse between the nations. The *Reichstag* will strongly promote the creation of international judicial organizations. However, as long as the enemy governments will not enter upon such a peace, as long as they threaten Germany and her allies with conquests and coercion, the German nation will stand together as a man and steadfastly hold out and fight until its own and its allies' right to life and development is secured. The German nation is invincible in its unity. The *Reichstag* knows that in this respect it is in harmony with the men who in heroic struggle are defending the Fatherland. The imperishable gratitude of the whole people is assured them.

(Gerald D. Feldman (ed.) *German Imperialism 1914–1918: The Development of a Historical Debate*, New York, Wiley, 1972, p. 42)

II.25 Extract from the diary of Hans Peter Hanssen (Nov. 1918)

[Hanssen was a *Reichstag* deputy representing North Schleswig, a province, with a large Danish minority, which had been taken from Denmark by the war of 1864. Hanssen was spokesman for the Danish minority during the war, which brought him into close contact with the SPD and especially with critics and opponents of the war. Following a plebiscite in 1920, much of Schleswig was returned to Denmark.]

Berlin, November 3, 1918. It is Sunday. At noon I was in the *Reichstag*. From the windows of the reading room I saw that a demonstration was taking place at Bismarck's statue. I went out on the balcony to hear the speeches. The Pan-Germans were giving a demonstration. They were passionately urging that peace negotiations be broken off and that the struggle be continued to the end. Patriotic songs were sung between speeches; *Deutschland, Deutschland, Die Wacht am Rhein, Heil Dir im Siegerkranz*. A noncommissioned officer jumped up on the pedestal and protested against the continuation of the war. The people became enraged. The police stepped in and carried him away.

As I was coming through the Siegesallee, a man fell unconscious directly in front of me. With the help of a passerby, I lifted him up on the pedestal beside the tomb of Kaiser Wilhelm. When he had regained consciousness, he whispered: 'Haven't had anything to eat since yesterday.' He was emaciated and half-dead from hunger. We saw to it that he received help.

There is much unrest in the working quarters. The Social Democratic press is using unusually sharp language against the Kaiser. Noske's articles in the *Chemnitzer Volksstimme* are helpful for the information they give. If the Kaiser does not abdicate soon, the Majority Socialists will be in a very difficult position.

On the whole it looks like a storm. While I was eating at Kempinski's this evening, I was seated at a table near two young men. They talked about the war. 'During the first year we were pleasantly led around by the nose,' said one bitterly. 'After being in the war for thirty-seven months without interruption,' said the other, 'my nerves are completely wrecked. I really live only when I can get alcohol. I have now only one desire: I was born a human being and want to be treated like a human being. But during the past four years I have been treated like an animal.'

A well-dressed gentleman and lady came and took a seat beside us. The gentleman joined in the conversation immediately. It turned out that he was a Rheinlander and had, like the others, participated in the war as a reserve officer. He had been severely wounded by a bullet which had gone straight through his head. 'Life is over for me,' he said indifferently; 'I now live only when I am drunk. The Kaiser ought to be shot and the military abolished! If a battle is called for that purpose, I'll go at once. One would have an opportunity to fight for a righteous cause.' The others eagerly gave their approval to the remark. When I expressed my astonishment at this strong language, they said to each other: 'That's the general attitude. In South Germany, it is much worse!'

Berlin, November 7, 1918. This morning, when I went to the *Reichstag* by a roundabout way, the streets presented a very warlike scene. Troops were marching in field equipment with shiny steel helmets. Street corners were occupied by strong military posts. Wherever it was possible to use a street strategically, windows in the upper stories of the buildings were dotted with machine guns. I passed several batteries. The artillery drove through the streets and made it plain that the cannon were ready for action, in order to show the citizens of Berlin what they may count on if they revolt. There is a foreshadowing of a bloody struggle. . . .

About five o'clock I returned to the *Reichstag*, where I met Ledebour.*
'You here?' I said, 'I thought you were at Kiel.'

He: 'No, we must divide up. We must also have people here in town.'

I: 'How are things going today?'

He: 'Kiel, Rendsburg, Hamburg, Lübeck, and Schwerin are in our hands. We are in control in Schleswig-Holstein, Mecklenburg, and the Hanse cities, but we will go further.'

I: 'What actually happened in Kiel?'

---

*Georg Ledebour, SPD journalist and editor, member of the *Reichstag*.

He: 'The Great Fleet was about to make an advance. The sailors declared: "We refuse to go. We will defend ourselves, but we will not attack under present conditions." Several hundred sailors were then arrested. The stokers on several ships put the fires out, and the sailors assumed control. The situation at Kiel, however, is still difficult, because the press, party officers, and the organizations still remain in the Government's socialist camp.'

I: 'What about things here?'

He: 'Our meeting tonight is forbidden, but that will only spread oil on the flames.'

I: 'Will anything happen tonight?'

He: 'No, we will not do anything. That would only cause deaths to no advantage. But we will soon have the upper hand. At a meeting which we held in Berlin last night I asked the gathering to drink to long life for the revolutionists, those brave seamen at Kiel. Scarcely had I made this request when the police lieutenant jumped up and broke up the meeting. I replied by shouting to the gathering: "The meeting is not dissolved; let us continue!" Then the police lieutenant laid hands on me and said: "You are under arrest; you will immediately come with me to headquarters!" "No!" I replied, "I shall go home when the meeting is over," and turned to the gathering: "Will some of you see to it that the lieutenant remains quiet while we proceed!" Many immediately assumed a threatening attitude, and a few men with clenched fists jumped up on the platform. This was sufficient. The lieutenant remained calm, and we resumed the proceedings. When I ended the meeting, he became courageous again and said: "You are under arrest, you will follow me to headquarters!" "No," I replied, "I will not follow you; I'm going home." And then to the audience: "Will you see that the gentleman remains here until I am gone?" I left the meeting, and the police did not dare to lay hands on me. In the meantime I did not go home, and it was a good thing that I didn't since the police came to my residence shortly afterwards to arrest me. Instead, I came here to the *Reichstag*, where they dare not violate my immunity.

'Thus we will go on. The police can support itself only upon a tottering authority. It no longer has any genuine power. And what authority it has left will soon be destroyed. We speak as we wish, and the guards see to it that the police will not touch us, and that we can again leave our quarters without being molested.

'The situation will now quickly come to a head. The revolution is marching in seven league boots. The socialist republic will soon be proclaimed. There is no other way out.'

(*Diary of a Dying Empire*, Port Washington, New York, Kennikat Press, 1973, pp. 339–40, 342–4)

II.26 Z. A. B. Zeman, from *The Break-up of the Habsburg Empire 1914–1918* (1961)

The longer the war lasts, the more strongly the simple question whether Austria–Hungary will be able to carry on the fight, not only in the military but also in the economic field, comes to the foreground. . . .

The reserves of troops are nearly exhausted, and we should expect that next spring Austria–Hungary will reach the limit of its military potential, though perhaps not in the sphere of production of armaments and ammunition, where surprising progress has been made under our leadership. The mood of depression here is increased – unfortunately not without justification – by the economic situation. This and the political measures concerning economy are simply impossible. There is no organization; when attempts were made to organize after our example, they ran into difficulties because of the local proclivity for 'muddling through', and because of an economy based on protection. No systematic work in this respect has been done, regulations were made without expert knowledge, and usually for one province at a time: such practices have led to a completely unjust distribution of provisions. The people in the suburbs of Vienna are starving; they are driven to despair by long queueing, which often brings no results . . . The situation has become still more serious since the poor results of this year's harvest in Austria and in Hungary, and also by the unsatisfactory economic relations between the two countries, which should, and this goes especially for Hungary, support each other loyally with food supplies. The Hungarian government, led by Count Tisza, pursues a Hungarian policy; in spite of high-minded phrases, it has no understanding of common needs and aims. Here, too, there is no personality that could dictate a policy which would safeguard common interests. . . .

I would like to point out that during the war, the relations between the two parts of the monarchy have deteriorated considerably. Although the feeling of common interest had seemed, at the beginning of the war, to have been strengthened by common danger, some time later exactly the opposite happened. Hungary in trying to loosen its ties with Austria more than ever before. Hungarian chauvinism is flourishing and one must admit that this is mainly Austria's fault. The many mistakes made by the Supreme Command – which is exclusively in Austrian hands – has embittered the Hungarians. The sins of Vienna's internal policy, committed during several decades, which have made the treason of the Czechs possible and for which many Hungarians have died, have also had their effect on the people in Hungary. . . . Magyar regiments are stationed in Bohemia in order to prevent unrest there, instead of being able to defend their fatherland. Recently, an Austrian politician has told me: 'Bohemia is in fact occupied by the Hungarians.' Nobody in Austria is prepared to introduce a new policy in the Czech lands: this was further illustrated when both the Czech members of the cabinet, who are ministers not because of their qualifications but because they represent their people, were elevated to the rank of baron. . . .

A similar [i.e. chaotic] situation can be observed in the financial field. Although the Minister of Finance has the best intentions of introducing order, he despairs because he cannot make the two Premiers introduce suitable measures. Germany pays its ally 100,000,000 marks every month, and apart from that it transfers to Austria regular subsidies for Bulgaria and Turkey; it is not impossible that the monarchy will present to us further bills in order to maintain the value of its currency. . . .

I believe that we should make an attempt to stabilize the situation here. We are running the danger that the Habsburg monarchy will suddenly sicken, and that Germany will share in its downfall.

(*The Break-up of the Habsburg Empire 1914–1918: A Study in National and Social Revolution*, Oxford University Press, 1961, pp. 96–7)

II.27 Otto Bauer, from *The Austrian Revolution* (1925)

[Dr Otto Bauer was Foreign Secretary in the First Republican Government of Austria.]

The social revolution which arose out of the war proceeded from the barracks rather than from the factories. When large numbers of soldiers and officers took part in the mass demonstration of the 30th October, when on this day the soldiers tore the imperial rosettes from their caps and forced the officers to do likewise, it was clear that military discipline in the Vienna barracks was completely undermined. The awful omnipotence with which the military organization had invested the officers during the war was transformed at one blow into absolute impotence. The four years' suppression of the dignity of the soldiers now revenged itself in a wild outburst of hatred of the man for the officer. Where blind obedience had hitherto reigned, an elemental, instinctive, anarchical revolutionary movement now set in. Crowds of soldiers, brought home from Russia, assembled near the Rossauer barracks and indulged in fiery speeches. They attempted to form a 'Red Guard'; they marched with rifles through the town; they seized ammunition waggons, and confiscated food stores. The officers themselves were caught up by the movement. Reserve officers recruited from the ranks of the intellectuals, infected with the revolutionary romanticism of Bolshevism, participated in the formation of the Red Guard, while German National officers held session in the Parliament Buildings as soldiers' councils. But the overwhelming majority of the soldiers were dominated by an irresistible desire to return home to wives and children. The Slav soldiers hastened home in disorderly fashion as soon as they had heard of the creation of national States in their countries. Their example immediately caused the German soldiers to join the desertion movement. The most important dépôts and magazines were left unguarded. Plundering began. The camps in which prisoners of war were interned were no longer guarded. For a few hours defenceless Vienna trembled at the imminent invasion of Italian prisoners of war from the Sigmundsherberg camp, who, after the desertion of the Austrian guards, had seized a magazine and proceeded to march against Vienna. No less great was the danger on the railways. There every train brought hungry and undisciplined armed soldiers returning from the Front. Shootings occurred daily at the railway stations, and the danger of the towns being plundered by Slav and Magyar soldiers, who were returning to their homes through Austrian territory, daily increased. Complete anarchy could only be obviated by the organization of a new defence force.

The Political Council tried first of all to enlist in its service what was left of the garrisons of the old army. And as the restoration of the authority of the officers seemed hopeless for the moment, the Political Council invited the men themselves to form soldiers' councils which would create order and discipline in the barracks. But these first efforts were unsuccessful. The soldiers took the oath and then rushed away to their wives and children. It was impossible to retain the reservists by the colours. There was only one thing to do: to recruit and organize a paid voluntary army. On the 3rd November, the day of the conclusion of the Armistice, the Political Council ordered that recruiting for the *Volkswehr* [militia] should commence. At this juncture Social Democracy made an effective use of its influence.

It was impossible to prevent the rapid demobilization of the old Army. The peasants' sons hastened back to their villages, to gorge themselves after four hungry years of war service. The *Volkswehr* was not calculated to attract the sons of the bourgeoisie. But the case was different with the industrial workers. The war industries had come to a standstill. Tens of thousands of men returning from the Front found no employment. Thus it came about that the battalions of the *Volkswehr* consisted almost exclusively of industrial workers. It must be admitted that most of these men were politically untrained, bestialized by the war, and ready for all kinds of political adventures. To place this force under strict discipline and protect it from the abuse of its political simplicity was now the task of Social Democracy.

Even during the war the ties between the comrades in the barracks and the party organization had never been quite severed. Comrades on leave consorted in labour institutes and brought their complaints to the party secretariat. In the summer of 1918, this loose connexion with the Vienna barracks was strengthened. Certain comrades were deputed to act as representatives in each body of troops. During the war this system kept us informed of everything that happened in the barracks. Now we were able to make use of these representatives to influence the organization of the *Volkswehr*. At the same time the party embarked upon an agitation in favour of this *Volkswehr*, which it sought to persuade old and reliable comrades to enter. Thus within the new battalions were formed *cadres* of organized Social Democrats, who imposed their leadership, and consequently that of the Party, upon the *Volkswehr*, inspiring it with socialist ideals, and restraining lawless and criminal tendencies.

The creation of the *Volkswehr* averted the threatened danger of anarchy from the country. The *Volkswehr* took over the guarding of dépôts and magazines. Battalions of the *Volkswehr* beat off attacks of Czech and Magyar troops who were being transported home through Austrian territory. The *Volkswehr* absorbed the Red Guard and compelled it to submit to its discipline and command. The force that was now deputed to guard the security of the country was a body of troops led by Social Democrats, marching with red flags to the strains of the *Marseillaise*.

The creation of the *Volkswehr* was a revolutionary act, indeed, the first act of the proletarian revolution which was beginning to overshadow the national revolution.

In the classic revolutions of the past, events were decided by the struggles at the barricades. By victory at the barricades the Revolution disarmed the powers of the old régime and called its own armed forces into existence. What used to be accomplished at one blow in a barricade fight was divided into two acts in the Austrian Revolution. The disarming of the old régime was carried out by the spontaneous dissolution of the Imperial armies. The armed power of the new régime took its rise in the *Volkswehr*. While in other revolutions the transference of power from the hands of the old to those of the new régime could never be effected without bloody civil war, we were here able to carry out this change, after the dissolution of the Army, as a mere work of organization through the creation of the *Volkswehr*. The Imperial Army was replaced by the Republican Militia, and this Republican force was a proletarian army inspired by the ideal of Socialism.

This revolution in the barracks immediately provoked a revolution in the factories. During the war, industrial enterprise had placed the workers under the immediate control of the military power; military managers had commanded in the factories, and military guards had kept the workers in awe. Now the whole authority of private enterprise and its organs crumbled to pieces with the collapse of the military power. The self-consciousness and the self-reliance of the workers were powerfully reinforced. The menacing agitation in the centres of labour intimidated the bourgeois parties and procured their submission to the will of Social Democracy. Thus the revolution proceeded on its course.

An actual Republican constitution had already been given to Austria on the 30th October, but the Emperor still remained in Vienna without renouncing the Throne. Early in November, the State secretaries appointed by the Political Council, had taken over those branches of the Imperial Ministries which were concerned with the administration of Austrian territory. But the departments which administered the institutions and domains of the Empire continued to exist by their side as 'liquidating' ministries. In all the central offices, an Austrian State secretary appointed by the Political Council sat beside an Austrian minister appointed by the Emperor. This duality of republican and monarchical administration in the same building was anomalous. It became intolerable when the Empire in neighbouring Germany collapsed. When Germany became a republic on the 9th November, the republican movement among the Austrian workers pressed for the removal of the last vestiges of the monarchical order. On the following day the representatives of Social Democracy in the Political Council intimated to the bourgeois that an armed rising of the workers and soldiers was inevitable if the proclamation of the Republic was delayed any longer. The bourgeois parties impressed by the strength of the movement in the barracks and in the factories, abandoned their opposition on the 11th November, when a decision of the Tyrolese National Council in favour of the Republic and reports from Upper Austria and from Carinthia indicated that a powerful republican movement was sweeping through the peasantry in these districts. The majority of the Political Council decided to convene the Provisional National Assembly to meet on the 12th November, and to submit to it the draft proclamation of the Republic. Advised by Lammasch, the Emperor now abandoned all opposition. On the 11th November, the last Habsburg formally laid down the government.

'Now, as always,' so ran the Emperor's proclamation, 'filled with unchanging love for my peoples, I will not place my person in the way of their free development. The people through their representatives have taken over the government. I renounce any further share in the business of the State.'

During this month of October, the idea of the Republic had been associated with the idea of union with Germany.

With the collapse of its rule over the other nations, German-Austria's historical mission was ended, for the sake of which she had hitherto willingly borne the separation from the German Motherland. The Germans in Bohemia, Silesia, Northern Moravia, and the German Alpine lands, separated by Czech territory, had no other choice than that between Czech alien rule, and union with Germany. How helpless Austria was on her own legs, when faced with the new national States, was discovered in the first stages of the Revolution. Austria was overtaken by hunger immediately the Czechs suspended the export of foodstuffs and coal. The first step which the nascent Austrian State was obliged to take was to request the Berlin Government to furnish assistance in the form of cereals.

Standing alone Austria could not possibly maintain her economic position in face of the hostility of the new national States. The economic losses caused by these national and territorial defections could only be compensated by the support of the economically stronger Empire. During October large sections of the middle classes, especially the intellectual classes, began to hope that union with Germany would offer some compensation for the collapse of their own edifice of domination.

On the other hand, the workers at that time received the idea of union somewhat coldly, although Social Democrats were its first sponsors. The workers had hated the German Empire during the war too thoroughly to be able to muster any enthusiasm for unity with this same Germany. Not until the 9th November did the unity movement capture the masses of workers. Not until the Empire in Germany was overthrown and a Socialist government, based on workers' and soldiers' councils, had seized power, when the German Revolution seemed with one powerful blow to have eclipsed ours, did it become patent to the workers that the great, highly-developed industrial Empire offered far more favourable conditions for the struggle to realize Socialism than the small territory of German-Austria, in helpless dependence upon neighbouring agrarian countries and half-agrarian itself.

The quarrel between Habsburg and Hohenzollern had estranged Austria from Germany. Now that the rule of Habsburg and Hohenzollern had simultaneously collapsed, the union of the race into one community seemed the natural consequence of the overthrow of the dynasties.

The Armistice on the basis of Wilson's fourteen points, which promised all peoples the right of self-determination, had just been concluded. If Austria was to attempt to effect a union with Germany, equipped with no other weapon than the appeal to the promised right, then unity could not remain the dream of individuals or the programme of parties: the Austrian nation had to demonstrate that at the same time as it demanded its freedom and took its fate into its own hands, it was also unanimous in setting the goal of unity before it.

Therefore, the representatives of Social Democracy in the Political Council proposed that the project of unity should be announced at the same time as the Republic. This proposal was accepted on the 11th November. On the following day the Provisional National Assembly held its third sitting. The legislative enactments of this day comprehended the salient features of the great transformation. Austria was declared a Republic. All the rights of the Empire were transferred to the Political Council; all the privileges of the House of Habsburg were abolished; all associations based upon political privileges – the delegations, the House of Lords, the diets and municipalities elected by a census suffrage – were dissolved. Elections to the Constituent National Assembly and new elections to the diets and municipalities based upon the equal suffrage of citizens, without distinction of sex, and proportional representation, were ordered to be held. The Republic, the abolition of political franchise privileges in the provinces and municipalities, female suffrage, and proportional representation were the achievements of the Democratic Revolution. This same legislative enactment also pushed the National Revolution to its logical conclusion. 'German-Austria,' declared article 2, 'is a constituent part of the German Republic.'

This closing chapter of the democratic and national revolution was the first phase of the social revolution, the change in the relative position of the classes, that had taken place. For it was the will of the working classes which had imposed the Republic upon the possessing classes. On the 21st October, at the first sitting of the Provisional National Assembly, the two great bourgeois parties had declared in favour of a constitutional monarchy; on the 12th November at the third sitting of the Provisional National Assembly, trembling at the threatened rising of the proletariat, they both accepted the Republic.

On the 12th November the working classes suspended work. While the Provisional National Assembly was holding session in the hall of the House of Lords, the Vienna working classes assembled in front of the Parliament buildings. This gigantic demonstration revealed the powerful social agitation among the masses.

In April, 1919, the Republican Government declared the 12th November, the day when the democratic and national revolution was completed, to be a public festival. But the middle classes have never participated in this public festival, which they regard as the anniversary of their capitulation to the proletariat. On the other hand, the working classes celebrate this day every year as the anniversary of their victory. This fact has a deep historical meaning. When the national policy of the bourgeoisie, the aim of which was the maintenance and strengthening of its rule over the other nations, was shattered, the leadership of the nation passed to the proletariat. The Austrian State was established under the intellectual guidance of Social Democracy. Yielding to the pressure of the working classes, it broke away from the Habsburg Empire, and renouncing all endeavours to effect union with the young and emancipated nations, embraced the idea of union with Germany. The national revolution became the cause of the proletariat, and the proletarian revolution became the custodian of the national revolution.

On the 12th November we had reached the point which the Left had indicated in January, 1918, as the first essential stages of the approaching Austrian Revolution, the point which the whole party, whose ranks closed up in face of the turn in world affairs, set before it in the first days of October as the immediate object to be achieved.

This object had been accomplished in the course of six weeks without street fighting and civil war, without using force or shedding blood. To be sure, like every other revolution, this one was a work of force. But the force which rendered the revolution possible was not expended in the streets of Vienna. On the battlefields, in the Balkans, and in Venetia, it smashed the obsolete mechanism which stood in the way of the revolution. Consequently, we were able to carry out the revolution at home without force. We were able to carry out the revolution because, during those decisive weeks from the 3rd October to the 12th November, we only demanded each day what was already ripe for the plucking, and only executed what could be accomplished without heavy sacrifice.

Thus, proceeding step by step, we finally achieved the whole of what we had set before us as our object. During these weeks, Victor Adler led the Party for the last time. His incomparable practical sense told him day by day what had become possible and, indeed, inevitable. His sense of responsibility would not allow us to try to take to-day at the cost of severe sacrifice what was bound to fall into our lap as ripe fruit to-morrow. His reputation, his humane understanding for the prostrate foe, facilitated the retirement of the vanquished. He died on the 11th November in sight of the accomplished task. He died at the moment when the education, the organization, and the strength of the Austrian working class, which were the results of his life's work, celebrated their greatest triumph; when the victory of the Party which he had united in his youth, which in manhood he had led to power, which he had preserved from disruption during his last years, was assured; when the national dream of his youth was coupled with the social work of his manhood, and he had bequeathed to the working class the great heritage of a revolutionary victory, not won with hand grenades or machine guns, but accomplished as an intellectual act, as the result of tactical and organizing skill, which enabled the revolution gradually to establish its empire over the minds of the people. . . .

The war brought about a fundamental change in the position and the mentality of the proletariat. It tore the workers away from the factories and places of work. In the trenches they suffered unspeakable things. In the trenches their souls were filled with hatred of the oppressors and the profiteers who had coined money out of popular necessity at home, while they looked death in the face every hour, and of the generals and officers who fared luxuriously while they starved. In the trenches they drank in greedily the narratives of returning soldiers who, as prisoners in Russia, had witnessed the first phase of the Russian Revolution, the phase of civil war, of bloody terrorism against officers, capitalists, and peasants, the phase of expropriations, requisitions, and nationalization. The years in the trenches had dulled their habits of work and accustomed them to requisitions and plundering, filling them with a belief in the efficacy of force. Now came the Revolution, and the day of returning home. But at home they found hunger, cold, and unemployment. The four years' accumulation of hatred and anger had to find an outlet. Now they would be revenged on those who had ill-treated them for four years. Now they would demand that the Revolution, which had expelled the Emperor, should pull down the mighty from their seats. Now they would see what the promised gratitude of the Fatherland to its heroes amounted to. And as they met with no other response than privation and misery, they believed that a few thousand resolute armed men would be able with one powerful blow to make an end of the social order which had brought war and need and misery upon them.

For four years military managers had commanded in the factories of the war industries. As labour discipline in the factories was based upon the military power, it dissolved when the latter collapsed. The industries lapsed into a state of chaos. All at once war orders ceased. The coal famine, lack of raw materials, the breakdown of labour discipline, disinclination for work on the part of a working class exhausted by the overwork of war-time and reduced by hunger and stirred to its inmost being by the events of the Revolution – all these were so many obstacles to the adaptation of production to peacetime conditions. The factories were transformed into debating forums. General industry was not able to absorb the workers who streamed out of the munition factories or returned home from the Front. The number of the unemployed mounted month by month. It reached its highest point in May, 1919. At that date there were 186,030 workless, of which 131,500 were in Vienna alone.

Wild excitement prevailed in the barracks of the *Volkswehr*. The *Volkswehr* was conscious of being the chief support of the Revolution. In the discussions within the soldiers' councils Social Democrats and Communists fought out their hardest battles. The *Volkswehr* thought that with its weapons in its hands, it could forthwith decide the victory of the proletariat. And among the wildly excited homecomers, among the despairing workless, among the militiamen filled with revolutionary romanticism, were disabled soldiers who wanted to avenge their personal injuries upon the guilty social order, were neurotic women whose husbands had languished in war captivity for years; were intellectuals and literary men of all kinds who, suddenly converted to Socialism, were filled with the Utopian radicalism of the neophyte; were Bolshevist agitators sent home from Russia. Every edition of the newspaper brought news of the struggles of Spartacus in Germany. Every speech announced the glory of the great Russian Revolution, which with one stroke had abolished exploitation for ever. The masses, who had just seen the overthrow of the once so powerful Empire, recked nothing of the strength of Entente Capitalism; they believed that the Revolution would now wing its way to the victorious countries. 'Dictatorship of the proletariat.' 'All power to the councils.' These were the cries that now resounded through the streets.

The workers' councils in Austria arose out of the January Strike. When the Revolution came, the young institution rapidly spread. The heightened consciousness of power, the awakened impulse to activity of the liberated masses sought and found in this institution their first field of activity. Economic necessity provided the direction to this active impulse. The workers' councils joined with the soldiers' councils and the peasants' councils which were coming into existence, to form local and district economic commissions. They controlled the garnering of the harvest and the rearing of cattle, the requests for and the allocation of dwellings. They attempted to terrorize the profiteer. They prevented the exportation of food from their districts. As a rule they co-operated with the legal authorities; in theory the authorities used the workers' councils as their organs of control; in reality the authorities were dictated to by the councils. At times, however, the councils acted independently and in opposition to the authorities.

In the first months of the revolution the movement was elemental and unorganized. As yet there was no cohesion between the workers' councils of the various districts. The movement was most widely spread in Upper Austria, where the workers' councils were instrumental in prohibiting external trade and defending the extremely rich stores of wheat and cattle from the activities of the illicit traders of Vienna.

It was not alone the urban and industrial workers who were revolutionized by the war. There was a great upheaval among the masses of peasants. But from the beginning this movement was of an ambiguous character. The peasants also had returned home from the trenches filled with hatred of war and militarism, bureaucracy and plutocracy. They, too, hailed the new-found freedom, the Republic, and the overthrow of militarism. It was a real democratic movement which at that time surged through the peasantry. But the peasant democracy is not identical with the proletarian democracy.

In the mind of the peasant the new-found freedom, which he as well as the worker wanted to employ, shaped into a determination which was in diametrical opposition to the needs of the proletariat.

During the war the enormous military requisitioning apparatus had weighed upon the peasantry with terrible force. It had destroyed the most valuable property of the Alpine peasantry, their cattle. The peasants' hatred of this requisition system made them revolutionaries. Compulsion to sell the products of their labour below the market price seemed to them a form of plunder which the revolution must abolish. The freedom which the peasants expected from the revolution which had destroyed militarism was first and foremost freedom from the oppressive war administration.

But the revolution was bound to disappoint this expectation. At a time of the direst need, it could not dispense with the centralized system of requisitioning and distributing food. The feeding of the towns and the industrial centres, above all the feeding of Vienna, could not have been effected without State regulation and control. The peasant saw that the revolution denied him what he understood by freedom. He saw that the military requisition detachments had been supplanted by workers' councils which enforced the delivery of supplies, hunted down illicit trade, and combated the infraction of the maximum price regulations. The peasant saw in the proletariat the enemy who refused to allow him the free disposal of the products of his labour. The peasant now began to hate the proletariat as formerly he had hated militarism.

The hostile sentiments of the peasantry towards the proletariat were encouraged by the urban middle class and the priesthood. The urban trading class was a natural ally of the peasantry against the central system of regulating food distribution. The urban bourgeoisie looked to the peasant masses for support against the proletariat. The priests reinforced and organized the peasant movement as the strongest bulwark against the proletarian revolution. Newspapers and sermons told the peasant that his corn, his cattle, and his wood were requisitioned for the purpose of allowing a hundred thousand workless men in Vienna to be kept in idleness by the State; that the central system of control which oppressed the peasant was maintained by an alliance of Jewish profiteers in the centres with the Jewish Labour leaders in the Government; that the revolution aimed at socializing his property and destroying his church.

The peasant proceeded to adopt a defiant attitude. He placed obstacles in the way of delivering supplies. Peasants' councils struggled with workers' councils for mastery of the administrative machinery. And the peasant knew that he was stronger. He had plenty of food in his cupboard, and he could blockade the town. If it came to civil war, it was not the peasant, but the worker who would starve. The peasant did not lack arms. When the army had melted away, the returning soldiers had sold their rifles to the peasants or left them to the peasants as booty.

With the antagonism of the peasantry to the working class, the antagonism of the countryside to Vienna was closely associated.

Prior to the revolution, Vienna was chiefly dependent upon the supplies drawn from the Sudetic district, Galicia, and Hungary. When these sources of supply were cut off, Vienna was obliged to draw far more food, fuel, and raw materials than formerly from the districts of Inner Austria, and this at a time when the production of Vienna had almost stopped owing to the lack of coal and raw materials, when Vienna was unable to offer any return to the districts whose agricultural produce it required. These districts, which were themselves suffering from a shortage of all necessary commodities, opposed the demands which Vienna made upon them. The initiative in this opposition was taken by the workers themselves. Workers' councils prevented foodstuffs from leaving the localities. Their organs of control guarded the railway lines. This policy was supported by the peasantry, to whom the detested system of control which the Republic maintained seemed a requisition system designed to plunder the countryside for the benefit of Vienna.

The new autonomous local governments which had emerged from the revolution became the centres of this economic particularism.

As the State government was compelled to combat the economic separation of the provinces, it came into sharp conflict with the local governments. The latter refused to obey the directions which came from Vienna. The bourgeoisie encouraged the opposition of the provinces to the State government. In the provinces where industry was weak, they found among the peasant majority a firm bulwark against the State government, which was dominated by the Vienna proletariat. If the elemental action of the workers' councils themselves had consolidated the economic exclusiveness of the provinces, it was now this provincial exclusiveness which enabled the bourgeoisie, supported by the peasantry, to commence to entrench itself against the concentrated strength of the proletarian revolution in Vienna.

Austria is divided into two areas nearly equal in population. On the one hand is the great industrial district, which comprises Vienna and a quarter of the Wienerwald and Upper Styria; on the other hand is the great agrarian region which includes all the other provinces. In the great industrial district all actual power was in the hands of the proletariat. In the great agrarian region, in which only a few populous towns and industrial centres are scattered over the countryside, the proletariat was not quite powerless, but the peasantry formed the strongest power and could not be suppressed. It was impossible to govern the great industrial district in opposition to the workers, but it was equally impossible to govern the great agrarian district in opposition to the peasants. The economic structure of the country therefore created an equilibrium between the strength of classes, which could only have been abolished by force in bloody civil war. Large sections of the proletariat were eager for such a civil war. The proletariat in Vienna, in Wiener-Neustadt, and in Donawitz, could not see beyond its powerful position in the industrial region. It was oblivious to the unshakeable power of the peasantry in the agrarian region, and was equally blind to the menacing power of Entente imperialism outside. Consequently, it considered the establishment of the dictatorship of the proletariat to be possible.

But the establishment of such dictatorship would have been nothing less than the suicide of the revolution. In the great industrial district the proletariat could have set up its dictatorship without encountering insuperable opposition. In the great agrarian region this attempt would have failed. The provinces would have answered the proclamation of dictatorship by separating from Vienna, by breaking away from the State. The struggle against the counter-revolution in the provinces would then have inevitably led to bloody civil war. But civil war would have provoked the intervention of the Entente. The Entente Powers could not have tolerated the interruption by civil war of communications in a country which provided their passage from the Adriatic to Czechoslovakia and Poland. They were determined not to allow the revolution to develop beyond the limits of democracy. Had the 'peace and order' which they desiderated been destroyed, they would have stopped the food trains and the coal trains and thus brought famine upon the whole industrial district; they would have given permission to the Czechs and the Jugo Slavs to march and thus have involved us in war; they would have caused the most important railway junctions and towns to be occupied by Italian troops and thus made an end of the revolution. The dictatorship of the proletariat would have ended with the dictatorship of foreign commanders.

Large sections of the proletariat did not realize these dangers. It was the duty of Social Democracy to see them. Thus a double task devolved upon Social Democracy; on the one hand, by taking advantage of the powerful revolutionary agitation among the masses and the severe shocks which the capitalist social order had suffered, to capture for the proletariat the strongest and most permanent positions in the State and in the workshop, in the barracks and in the schools; but on the other hand, to prevent this revolutionary agitation from developing into civil war and open collision with the superior forces of Entente imperialism, which would have opened the gates to famine, invasion, and counter-revolution.

If the struggle of the classes for power was not to be conducted and decided by force of arms, it had to be fought out under the forms of democracy. Consequently, our first task was to organize the elections to the Constituent National Assembly. The elections took place on the 16th February, 1919. As a matter of fact, they could only be held in Inner Austria, as the German districts of the Sudetic provinces had already been occupied by the Czechs. For the Social Democrats 1,211,814 votes were cast; for the Christian Socialists 1,068,382, and for the German National Parties 545,938. Of the 159 seats, 69 fell to the Social Democrats, 63 to the Christian Socialists, and 24 to the German National Parties, which henceforth called themselves Pan-Germans. The German Nationalists, who were the strongest party in the Provisional National Assembly, became the weakest party in the Constituent National Assembly; the Social Democrats, the weakest of the three great parties in the Provisional National Assembly, became the strongest party in the Constituent National Assembly. To be sure we lacked an absolute majority in the newly-elected parliament. We should have been able to capture a majority, if industrial German Bohemia could have voted with us; the Czech occupation of German Bohemia saved to the bourgeoisie and the peasantry the majority in the Austrian National Assembly. But if we did not have the majority, we were still the strongest party, and the direction of the new parliament devolved on us.

In the first place the elections were a popular pronouncement upon Monarchy *versus* Republic. The verdict was unequivocal. In its first enactment the newly elected National Assembly solemnly repeated the decisions of the 12th November: the proclamation of Austria as a democratic Republic and union with Germany. On the 11th November, Karl Habsburg had promised to submit to the decision of the Austrian people as to their political constitution. Renner intimated to the ex-Emperor that he could only remain in Austria if he fulfilled his promise to renounce the throne for himself and his House. Karl Habsburg demurred to the abdication demanded of him, and on the 23rd March departed, under English protection, for Switzerland. The National Assembly replied to this gesture by passing the law of the 2nd April, 1919, which banished all members of the House of Habsburg from the country and confiscated their family possessions for the benefit of disabled soldiers.

At the same time the National Assembly proceeded to consolidate the Republic. In November the Provisional National Assembly had itself taken over the burden of power; its executive organ, the Political Council chosen from all parties, had been the proper government, the State Secretaries being merely its organs. This constitution, which provided for the governing Political Council through the selection of members of the parties on the principle of proportional representation, was adapted to the needs of the time of State-building, which required the co-operation of all parties, of 'bourgeois, peasant, and worker.' It was no longer appropriate at a time when the class antagonisms had developed further and had divided parliament into governing majority and Opposition upon the basis of the State already constituted. Consequently, the Political Council was abolished by the enactment of the 14th March. Some of its functions were transferred to the President of the National Assembly, who at the same time assumed the duties of President of the Republic. Seitz was chosen as first President. But the proper powers of government were transferred to the State Government, which was henceforth directly chosen by Parliament. With this the period of the co-operation of all parties was over. Henceforth, it was a question of forming a majority inside Parliament which would elect and support the Government.

At that time the Government was still confronted with the passionate demonstrations of the returned soldiers, the workless, and the war invalids. It was confronted with a *Volkswehr* filled with the spirit of the proletarian revolution. It was daily confronted with serious and menacing conflicts in the factories and on the railways. And the Government had no coercive agencies at its command. Armed force was not an instrument to use against proletarian masses filled with revolutionary ardour. Only by daily appeals to the intelligence, the proper feelings of responsibility of hungry and freezing masses stirred by war and revolution, could the Government prevent the revolutionary movement from culminating in a civil war which would destroy the revolution. No bourgeois government could have grappled with this task. It would have been defenceless against the mistrust and hatred of the proletarian masses. It would have been overthrown in a week by street insurrection, and imprisoned by its own soldiers. Only Social Democrats could grapple with this unprecedentedly difficult task. Only they were trusted by the proletarian masses. Only they could convince the masses that the terrible privations of this first winter after the war were not the fault of the Government, but the unavoidable consequence of the world-wide transformation; that they could not be evaded by a forcible upheaval, but only gradually be overcome. Only Social Democrats could procure the ending of wildly excited demonstrations by negotiations and discussions, only Social Democrats could pacify the unemployed, direct the *Volkswehr*, and restrain the workers from the temptation to embark upon revolutionary enterprises which would have been fatal to the revolution. The functions which at that time were the most important functions of the Government could only be fulfilled by Social Democrats. The severe blows which had been dealt to the bourgeois social order found their most striking expression in the fact that a bourgeois government, a government without Social Democrats, was downright impossible.

But a purely social democratic government was just as impossible as a purely bourgeois government. Little as the great industrial district of Vienna, Wiener-Neustadt and Upper Styria would have tolerated a purely bourgeois government, just as little would the great agrarian district of the provinces have tolerated a purely social-democratic government. A purely social-democratic government would have lost all influence upon the provincial governments; it would not have been able to prevent the breaking away of the provinces; it would have been powerless in face of the open resistance of the peasantry. Without a majority in Parliament, it would have had recourse to dictatorial methods, and would thereby have inevitably provoked civil war, in which the revolution would have been submerged.

No government was possible without the representatives of the workers. No government was possible without the representatives of the peasants. A common government of the workers and the peasants was the only possible solution. It was incumbent upon the workers and peasants to come to an understanding in the government and to endeavour to rule together, if they were not within a short time to face each other in open civil war.

In the country the Christian Socialists were the mass party of the peasants. The peasant representatives, who formed the overwhelming majority of the Christian Socialist deputies, were under the influence of the powerful agitation that was surging through the peasantry. The divergent character of this movement determined the policy of the Christian Socialist representatives. Against the dictatorship of the proletariat they would have summoned the peasantry to civil war. Upon the basis of a radical, republican, anti-militarist and anti-plutocratic democracy they desired to co-operate with the proletariat. Quite different were the sentiments of the Christian Socialist deputies of the urban, especially the Viennese, bourgeoisie. To the bourgeoisie the revolution signified nothing else than the collapse of its domination in municipality and factory, and its subjection to the might of the workers. Consequently, its sentiments were openly of a counter-revolutionary character, and it was quite under the influence of monarchical circles: of the high clergy, the clerical nobility, the counter-revolutionary officers. While the Christian Socialist peasant representatives, in common with the Social Democrats, advocated the punishment of the war crimes of generals and officers, the urban Christian Socialists adopted the rôle of protectors and defenders of these officers. In the debates upon the laws concerning the banishment of the Habsburgs, the confiscation of their property, and the abolition of titles of nobility, peasant and urban Christian Socialists were often found in opposite camps. The influence of the Church was strong enough to prevent the split in the Christian Socialist Party which had been threatening for a time, but the division in the Christian Socialist Party was sufficiently marked to enable us to come to an understanding with its peasant Wing. The co-operation of the workers and the peasants found its parliamentary expression in the coalition of Social Democrats with the Christian Socialist Party dominated by its peasant majority.

But within this coalition the forces were by no means of equal strength. The powerful revolutionary movement among the workers put the peasantry on the defensive; thus, within the proletarian-peasant coalition, the party of the proletariat was by far the stronger partner. This distribution of power within the coalition was reflected in the composition of the coalition Government which was formed on the 15th March, 1919. All the State offices which were concerned with the administration of the State were allotted to Social Democrats: Renner became Chancellor and Home Secretary; Deutsch was Minister for War, and I was Foreign Secretary. Hanusch became Secretary for Social Welfare. I took charge of the Socialization Commission which was set up. With the formation of the first coalition Government the working class captured not indeed supreme power, but predominant power in the Republic. . . .

Unlike other governments, the coalition Government could not enforce obedience; it could only rule by appealing to the intelligence of the masses, and explaining to them the position of the country.

In order to influence the masses, the Government had to act in close co-operation with the great social organizations. As nothing but the influence of the soldiers' committees upon the militiamen guaranteed obedience to the orders of the War Minister, the latter could not conduct his departmental business except in constant consultation with soldiers' committees. As nothing but the influence of the trade unions and the personal representatives of the railwaymen, the postmen, the telegraph and telephone employees guaranteed the undisturbed maintenance of communications, the Minister for Communications could not fulfil the functions of his office except in the closest co-operation with the trade unions and personal representatives. When supplies of food and coal ceased, when the workers here and there rebelled against the fearful economic conditions, it was only the works' committee that could pacify the excited masses; consequently the Home Secretary could not transact the business of his office except upon the closest understanding with the works' committees. Similarly, the Social Welfare Ministry and the Food Ministry could only be administered in the closest co-operation with the trade unions and the co-operative societies respectively. In this way the organizations in question gained a decisive influence upon the whole of the State administration. The Government was compelled to act upon the principle that no legislation could be embarked upon except in agreement with the organization of those immediately affected by it.

One effect of this was an alteration in the functions of the organizations. If the organizations were parties to decisions upon important activities of government, they were obliged to assume responsibility for these acts before their members. If the organizations in the course of their daily negotiations with the Government secured all the concessions that were possible, it was incumbent on them to resist impossible demands from their members. In this way Social Democracy, the trade unions, the works' committees and the soldiers' councils became partners in administration and organs of governmental power at the same time.

The structure of Social Democracy and of the trade unions was wholly transformed. The revolution brought them multitudes of recruits. In January, 1913, Social Democracy had 91,000 members in the German districts of Inner Austria. In January, 1919, the number was 332,391. In the year 1913 the trade unions had 253,137 members in the same area, but 772,146 members in the year 1919. Two-thirds of the party and trade union membership were new recruits. The apathetic workers who, prior to the war, had taken no part in the Labour Movement; the subservient workers who before the war had been forced into the yellow trade unions by the factory feudalism; the employees who before the war had kept themselves aloof from the workers – all of these now streamed into the party and the trade unions. The organizations were full of untrained and inexperienced members.

The alteration in structure produced a corresponding alteration in the functions of the party and the trade unions. Before and during the war our most important task was to revolutionize the sentiments of the masses. During and after the revolution an entirely different task confronted us. Now it behoved us to teach the masses, whom the collapse of the old machinery of domination had flooded with a consciousness of their strength, to make cautious use of their power. We had now to prevent the workers, brutalized by four years of war, from being demoralized by the newly-won freedom and led into courses of unbridled violence. We had to save the masses from being seduced by the illusions created by the revolution into deeds which would have brought disaster upon them. The new task was easy where we had to deal with our old members, who were trained by a decade of struggles, and inspired by confidence in our leadership. It was incomparably more difficult where we had to deal with a multitude of new recruits lacking all political and trade union training.

The machinery of government functioned in the following manner: all important governmental actions were concerted by the social democratic members of the Government with the leaders of the great Labour organizations, with the directive organs of the party, of the trade unions, and of the workers' and soldiers' councils. Then it was the task of the social democratic members of the Government to pilot these decisions through the coalition Government and the National Assembly. The leaders of the Labour organizations had to gain the support of the masses for the policy which they had arranged with the members of the Government. First of all the leaders of the Labour organizations had to gain the assent and co-operation of the delegates of the party and the trade unions, and of the workers' and soldiers' councils. Then these delegates had to perform the difficult and important task of enforcing the policy of the organizations in works and barracks meetings before the masses themselves. At such meetings the wildly excited masses were confronted with a party delegate, a works' committee, or a soldiers' committee upon the platform. The audience would be dissatisfied. They would demand more than the delegate could bring them. They would clamour for violent decisions. The delegate would speak of the economic necessities of the Republic, of its dependence upon foreign countries, of the superiority of the foreign capitalist powers. In the hall would be hunger, despair, passion. On the platform, appreciation of economic possibilities, perception of the international limits of the revolution, exhortation to caution, and appeals to the sense of responsibility. It was a severe struggle; a struggle which imposed on the delegates not merely the highest intellectual, but also the highest moral, demands. For the sake of the cause at stake, they had to face their own comrades fearlessly, to bear calumnies, complaints, and sometimes even threats and mishandling from the excited masses, and in the end carry out the policy that had been adopted as the only practical one. Friedrich Adler, whose revolutionary deed had gained him the greatest popularity, said at this time: 'Popularity is capital which has only to be employed for this purpose to be consumed.' Not merely a few dozen party and trade union delegates, but many thousands of modest delegates, works' committees, workers' and soldiers' councils have acted upon this high moral principle.

In works' meetings and barracks' meetings of this kind the great temptation of Bolshevism was repulsed, and the restoration of the relaxed labour discipline was gradually accomplished. In such works' meetings irresponsible strikes were averted, and discipline and order restored, when hunger and excitement had led the masses into courses of violence and excess. The history of works' meetings and barracks' meetings in the inner, intellectual history of the Austrian Revolution, and its secret history so far as the bourgeoisie is concerned, which scarcely noticed, certainly never understood, this great process of the intellectual self-mastery of the working class.

In the American Declaration of Independence of 1776, democracy was defined as a system of government conducted with the assent of the governed. Never and nowhere has democracy in this sense been more completely realized than in this first phase of the Austrian Revolution. For its government, lacking all means of coercing the governed, could not govern at all except by laboriously procuring, daily and hourly, the assent of the governed. These methods of government were imposed on it by the weakness of the State power which emerged from the revolution. It was obliged to attempt to govern by these methods under the most unfavourable conditions imaginable: at a time of extraordinarily severe mass privations, at a time of extraordinarily great mass excitement, at a time when a large section of the masses was demoralized by four years of war. The attempt could only succeed at the cost of many heavy sacrifices, even many intellectual sacrifices. But it did succeed. The fact of its success is the measure of the human greatness of the Austrian Revolution.

(*The Austrian Revolution*, trans. H. J. Stenning, Leonard Parsons, 1925, pp. 56–66, 83–97, 164–8)

DATE DUE
